IMAGES
of Rail

RAILS AROUND
HELPER

The town of Helper, Utah, bustles in the shadow of the massive Book Cliff mountain range in this 1972 photograph. Though the Denver and Rio Grande Western Railroad dominates the town, the vast coal reserves uncovered beneath these mountains determined the railroad's placement through Utah and helped the company and the town succeed.

ON THE COVER: Rio Grande Engine No. 843, a Class S-33 0-6-0, stands proudly in the Helper rail yards with her crew c. 1910. Joseph Stahr (second from left) was an engineer stationed out of Helper. On May 2, 1912, two of Stahr's small children were killed and his wife severely burned when a runaway train full of coal oil crashed into an engine idling near their house alongside the tracks in Helper. (Courtesy of the Western Mining and Railroad Museum.)

IMAGES
of Rail

RAILS AROUND
HELPER

SueAnn Martell and the
Western Mining and Railroad Museum

ARCADIA
PUBLISHING

Published by Arcadia Publishing
Charleston, South Carolina

Library of Congress Catalog Card Number: 2007924636

For all general information contact Arcadia Publishing at:
Telephone 843-853-2070
Fax 843-853-0044
E-mail sales@arcadiapublishing.com
For customer service and orders:
Toll-Free 1-888-313-2665

Visit us on the Internet at www.arcadiapublishing.com

To my grandfathers James A. Greener, whose many railroad stories will live on, and Jack Marchello, whom I know only through pictures. And to my father, George A. Martell, who shared his love of trains and the Rio Grande with me.

CONTENTS

ACKNOWLEDGMENTS

When Helper resident Fred Voll began the Western Mining and Railroad Museum in 1963, I am certain that he did not realize how much the museum would grow. In the 44 years since the museum was born, it has grown to display four floors of artifacts, include three outdoor display areas, and maintain over 5,000 historic photographs. As the director of this world-class institution, I am proud to be a part of a long line of dedicated people who have helped to keep this fascinating history alive. My thanks go out to each and every one of them—without their love and passion, this book would have never been possible.

I would like to extend a special thank-you to the Museum Advisory Board for the opportunity to use the museum collections in this work. Unless otherwise noted, all of the images were provided by this incredible collection. Thanks also goes to the museum's wonderful staff of volunteers, who never cease to amaze me with their knowledge, their accomplishments, and the fact that while I might write about the history, they lived it.

I would also like to thank the Western Mining and Railroad Museum's assistant director Amanda V. Maddox for providing additional photographs from her own collection, the stories of her family at Thistle and Soldier Summit, as well as for her never-ending encouragement.

My thanks also goes out to my fiancé, Darrin Teply, not only for his efforts to scan and prepare all of the images for this book, but also for his unconditional love and support even when the photographs had the wrong numbers and he had to help identify dozens of locomotives by their nearly invisible numbers in 100-year-old photographs. Also, my heartfelt thanks goes to Darrin's parents, Jim and Judith Teply, for their support and encouragement.

Last but not least, I would like to thank my family: my parents, the late George and Maurine Martell, who taught me how to appreciate the world around me—both past and present—and my aunt, Virginia Cochrane, who has always pushed me to do my best in everything.

INTRODUCTION

To visit the railroads of Helper, Utah, is to experience some of the most remarkable mountain railroading anywhere. From steep grades to a wide variety of train traffic, these lines offer something for everyone to enjoy. While the scenery around Helper is vastly different from that of other mountain railroads, it is no less striking. The bare rock and high windswept valleys makes one wonder why the railroad built here and how they did it.

To find the answer, one must realize that the history of the railroads of Helper is multifaceted. It is impossible to discuss the railroads of eastern Utah without also discussing the coal-mining industry. The two are inextricably linked. It was the vast coal deposits of the area that prompted the Denver and Rio Grande to move its easier, more southerly route to Salt Lake City to the more direct but nearly impassable route through Price Canyon.

It is impossible to discuss the railroads of the region without a discussion of the town of Helper itself. Although founded by Mormon settlers, Helper was built by the railroad and as such maintains a strong and distinct railroad identity, much different from any other town in Utah. Helper's rowdy ways and rebellious nature led to criticism from the more "proper" towns in the state that Helper had more bars and brothels than churches. This statement held true until well into the 1970s, with Helper being a loud and boisterous black sheep in Utah's respectable and polite society.

It is also important to discuss the immigrants that flocked to Helper to find work on the railroad. Driven by troubles in their homelands, these immigrants sought a better life in America. They traveled to Helper with only as many things as they could carry, and the Denver and Rio Grande Western Railroad not only brought them West, it gave them hope. While the railroad may have attracted them to Helper, it did not always hold them as employees. Some of these immigrants left their lives on the railroad and built businesses. Helper became known as the "Town of '57 Varieties," a play off a famous national advertising campaign, and for a while, a large wooden "57" decorated a hillside in the Helper rail yards. Walking down Main Street was like traveling the world. Italians, Greeks, Yugoslavians, Germans, Japanese, Chinese, Hispanic, French, Scottish, Welch, and English were just a few of the more common cultures there. Even today, the descendants of these original immigrants celebrate life's milestones with a diverse mix of cultures. Keilbasa is served alongside lasagna, lamb stew, and homemade tamales, and accordion music rings out for the mandatory polka.

Helper was not the only railroad town in Utah's high desert. All along the tracks, towns large and small were created to keep the railroad running at peak efficiency. Although not the mecca for railroading that Helper was, these towns operated in support of the larger railroad dynamic. Unlike Helper, these towns succumbed to the hands of time and the advancement of technology to become only memories in the minds of those who once called them home.

The Denver and Rio Grande Western Railroad was also not the only railroad in Helper. Many of these railroads, including the Denver and Rio Grande Western, have faded into the past, taken over in recent years by the Union Pacific Railroad. Only one remains, mostly unchanged: the

7

Utah Railway. Beginning its life like so many others, the Utah Railway was almost destined to be crushed by the larger and more powerful Denver and Rio Grande. Instead, the Utah Railway triumphed over the giant and gained control over the coal lands of eastern Utah. Running on rails that have remained basically unchanged for almost 100 years, the Utah Railway is still a daily presence in Helper's rail yards.

It is said that to truly know a town, visit the cemetery; for here, one will find the past. For many, an area's past is also present in its photographs, which tell the true story behind the names, the dates, and the places. They capture the essence of the people, of their jobs, and of their lives, and they hold that moment forever.

While the railroads around Helper will never again be as they were in the early days, those times live on in the architecture, the photographs, the histories, and the people who strive to preserve the past. With the sound of the trains still singing through the valley, Helper continues to be one of the premier railroad towns in the West, a necessary destination for any diehard rail fan. More importantly, Helper is a town that put down deep roots, tamped down by the thundering weight of the rumbling locomotives—roots that refuse to budge and refuse to die.

One

THE RAILROAD COMES TO TOWN

In the late 1870s, the area surrounding Helper was a desolate, high desert that had attracted only a dozen or so hardy souls who tried to make a living off the land. Mormon polygamist Teancum Pratt answered the call to settle the region but found the area populated with "soreheads who did not welcome any settlers."

When the Denver and Rio Grande Railroad began looking to change its route from its proposed southerly direction to a more direct line to Salt Lake City, it was the discovery of the vast coal deposits of eastern Utah that made the choice for them. When railroad officials met with Pratt to discuss the sale of some of his lands, the discouraged Pratt, tired of failing at farming, readily sold a portion of his homestead.

Thinking that this was the end of his financial troubles, Pratt saw the coming of the railroad as a boon to his investment. Little did Pratt know that with the entry of the railroad into the little valley, his home would be changed forever as the railroad put down roots.

Unlike other parts of Utah, the newly formed town of Helper seemed to go against every principle that Utah was founded on. Gambling halls, saloons, and brothels sprung up overnight to profit from the hardworking men. Shootings were common, and outlaws hoping to make a little money the quick way were ever present in the infant city. Pratt's dream of a quiet, pious community was dashed. In his diary Pratt wrote, "They were not of the honest kind who will pull together and sacrifice for each other." But Pratt could not change Helper's destiny. Industry had begun to build the city, and it would be driven by the principles of that industry. By 1883, the railroad had come to town, and the rambunctious and rowdy town of Helper was born.

Helper's first settler was Teancum Pratt. A Mormon polygamist, Pratt and his two wives, Annie Eliza Mead and Sarah Elizabeth Ewell, filed homestead papers in late 1881. Pratt never succeeded with his new land. After spending time in prison for unlawful cohabitation, he tried his hand at coal mining. Pratt was killed on September 8, 1900, at the Winter Quarters coal mine, where he had gone to work for the winter.

Bordered by the small Price River and the newly completed railroad yards, Helper was picture-perfect in this *c.* 1884 photograph. Helper struggled as a farming community and was destined for failure without the introduction of the railroad. While several of the original settlers continued to farm, the railroad changed the future of Helper from agricultural to industrial.

Work on a railroad grade through central and southern Utah was under way when Denver and Rio Grande founder William Jackson Palmer made a play for a large coal deposit in eastern Utah. In 1881, railroad official M. T. Burgess chose a new, more challenging route through Price River Canyon to access these deposits. In this *c.* 1882 photograph, these men and their grading teams relax just south of Price.

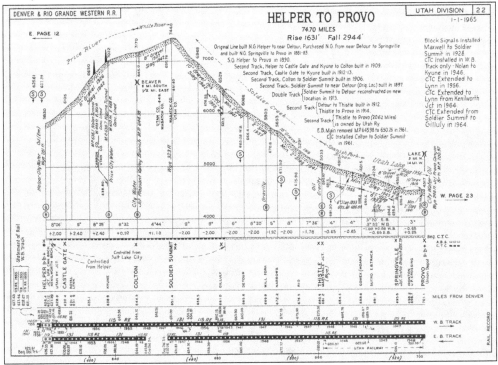

This elevation map shows the steep grade that this new route would conquer. Rising from an elevation of 5,830 feet at Helper to a summit of 7,440 feet, the railroad would climb 1,631 feet before falling 2,944 feet to the Utah valley, a distance of only 75 miles. This steep terrain required between 2- and 2.4-percent grades, a difficult climb for early steam engines. (Courtesy SueAnn Martell.)

By 1883, the Denver and Rio Grande Western Railroad had completed its narrow-gauge line from Green River to Helper. Originally called Pratt's Siding, the railroad soon changed the settlement's name to Helper in honor of the "helper" engines that were required for the steep grade. Though newspapers pleaded with the railroad to rethink the name change, this *c.* 1884 photograph shows the newly constructed depot with the name proudly displayed.

The August 21, 1891, issue of the *Eastern Utah Advocate* announced that the railroad would begin construction of a 30-stall roundhouse, improvements to the depot, and housing for employees at a cost of $50,000. One week later, the paper reported that construction had begun on the more manageable 15-stall roundhouse and that the total cost had dropped to $40,000. Construction on the project was completed in 1892, shortly before this photograph was taken.

As part of the 1892 construction project, the railroad built a hotel and a "beanery," or restaurant, pictured here. In the background, Helper's famous landmark, the Balanced Rock, is visible at the top of the mountain. By the early 1890s, the railroad yard was growing, and Helper had become a principal division point, halfway between Ogden, Utah, and Grand Junction, Colorado.

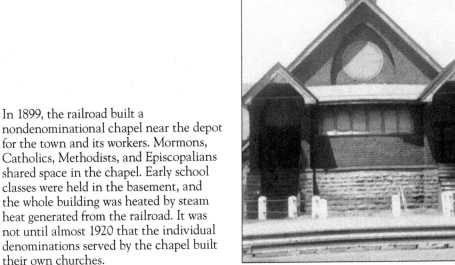

In 1899, the railroad built a nondenominational chapel near the depot for the town and its workers. Mormons, Catholics, Methodists, and Episcopalians shared space in the chapel. Early school classes were held in the basement, and the whole building was heated by steam heat generated from the railroad. It was not until almost 1920 that the individual denominations served by the chapel built their own churches.

One of the most dominant features of the Helper railroad yard was the coal tower, pictured here. Not only was coal the most common product carried by the Denver and Rio Grande Western on its main line from Helper to Salt Lake, but it was also necessary for the operation of the trains, as wood was scarce.

A young boy, his dog, and a businessman pose for the photographer c. 1898 near the railroad hotel and water tank. The depot is in the distance. The small engine has just left a maintenance shack on its way to the main yard track. Note the large platform in front of the hotel, which allowed passengers to get on and off the trains with ease.

The Helper landscape is dominated by the large sandstone cliff of Balanced Rock Mountain, part of the Book Cliff range. The railroad yards seem small by comparison in this 1892 photograph. The depot, the beanery, and the railroad hotel are visible, as is a cadre of cabooses and boxcars near the roundhouse (far right).

The engineer and fireman of this westbound passenger train pose for a photograph near the water tank while their passengers board the train c. 1899. The passengers are boarding in front of the railroad hotel at trackside. Note the extra "helper" engine between the lead engine and tender and the baggage car.

Denver and Rio Grande Railway

DENVER AND OGDEN LINE.

Westward: No. 49. Emigrant.	Westward: Pacific Express.	Local Time In effect Jan. 15, 1884.	Miles.	Eastward: Atlantic Express.	Eastward: No. 10. Emigrant.
8 30 p.m.	7 50 p.m.	Lv. Denver Ar.	.....	9 00 p.m.	7 15 a.m.
8 44 "	8 02 "	" Burnham Lv.	2	8 44 "	7 00 "
8 57 "	8 06 "	" N. O. Crossing "	4	8 39 "	6 50 "
9 18 "	8 15 "	" Petersburg "	8	8 29 "	6 18 "
9 30 "	8 22 "	" Littleton "	11	8 22 "	6 05 "
10 05 "	8 37 "	" Acequia "	17	8 09 "	5 23 "
10 43 "	8 52 "	" Sedalia "	25	7 53 "	4 40 "
11 04 "	9 02 "	" Mill No. 2 "	29	7 44 "	4 15 "
11 23 "	9 10 "	" Castle Rock "	33	7 35 "	4 00 "
11 35 "	9 17 "	" Douglas "	35	7 29 "	3 46 "
11 52 "	9 27 "	" Glade "	39	7 22 "	3 30 "
12 15 a.m.	9 39 "	" Larkspur "	43	7 14 "	3 07 "
12 45 "	9 52 "	" Greenland "	47	7 05 "	2 45 "
1 25 "	10 08 "	" Palmer Lake "	52	†6 54 "	2 13 "
1 52 "	10 16 "	" Monument "	56	6 33 "	1 52 "
2 09 "	10 24 "	" Borsta "	58	6 25 "	1 18 "
2 35 "	10 33 "	" Husted's "	62	6 16 "	12 50 "
3 05 "	10 43 "	" Edgerton "	67	6 04 "	12 13 a.m.
3 55 "	11 00 "	" Colorado Sp's. "	75	5 44 "	11 10 p.m.
4 45 "	11 18 "	" Widefield "	84	5 22 "	9 45 "
5 10 "	11 26 "	" Fountain "	89	5 13 "	9 20 "
5 40 "	11 38 "	" Little Buttes "	94	5 01 "	8 45 "
6 05 "	11 46 "	" Wigwam "	100	4 51 "	8 20 "
6 35 "	11 56 "	" Pinon "	106	4 40 "	7 43 "
7 08 "	12 08 a.m.	" Cactus "	112	4 28 "	7 17 "
7 35 "	12 18 "	" Nada "	117	4 15 "	6 45 "
*7 50 " 8 40 "	12 25 " 12 40 "	Ar./Lv. So. Pueblo Lv./Ar.	120	4 08 " 4 00 "	6 30 " *5 00 "
9 05 "	12 50 "	" Goodnight Lv.	124	3 50 "	4 32 "
9 30 "	1 00 "	" Meadows "	130	3 40 "	4 02 "
9 57 "	1 13 "	" Swallows "	135	3 30 "	3 30 "
10 22 "	1 25 "	" Carlile Springs "	140	3 18 "	2 48 "
10 37 "	1 30 "	" Beaver Creek "	143	3 11 "	2 29 "
10 42 "	1 32 "	" Thompson "	144	3 09 "	2 15 "
11 15 "	1 52 "	" Florence "	152	2 50 "	1 30 "
12 10 p.m.	2 10 "	" Canon City "	161	2 32 "	12 50 "
12 20 "	2 17 "	" Grape Creek Junc. "	162	2 22 "	12 20 p.m.
1 10 "	2 45 "	" Parkdale "	171	1 55 "	11 30 a.m.
1 43 "	3 00 "	" Spike Buck "	176	1 43 "	11 00 "
2 40 "	3 22 "	" Texas Creek "	166	1 21 "	10 08 "
3 22 "	3 39 "	" Cotopaxi "	193	1 06 "	9 23 "
4 01 "	3 57 "	" Vallie "	199	12 52 "	8 49 "
4 34 "	4 09 "	" Howards "	205	12 41 "	8 12 "
4 48 "	4 14 "	" Badger "	207	12 36 "	7 58 "
5 35 "	4 32 "	" Cleora "	215	12 20 "	7 12 "
*5 45 " 6 40 "	4 40 " 4 48 "	Ar./Lv. Salida Lv./Ar.	217	*12 15 p.m. 11 55 a.m.	7 09 " *5 30 "
7 05 "	5 03 "	" Poncha Lv.	222	11 42 "	5 03 "
7 37 "	5 23 "	" Otto "	226	11 22 "	4 32 "
7 50 "	5 30 "	" Mears "	228	11 15 "	4 20 "
8 10 "	5 40 "	" Shirley "	230	11 05 "	4 05 "
9 00 "	6 09 "	" Gray's Siding "	236	10 40 "	3 22 "
9 35 "	6 27 "	" Pocono "	......	10 20 "	3 00 "
10 05 "	6 45 "	" Marshall Pass "	242	10 05 "	2 35 "
10 30 "	7 02 "	" Hillesden "	245	9 45 "	2 05 "
11 10 "	7 25 "	" Chester "	250	9 20 "	1 30 "
11 47 "	7 47 "	" Buxton "	254	8 57 "	1 00 "
12 25 a.m. 12 50 "	8 00 " *8 20 "	Ar./Lv. Sargent Lv./Ar.	259	8 40 " *8 20 "	12 25 " 12 05 a.m.
1 35 "	8 42 "	" Crooks Lv.	267	7 58 "	11 18 p.m.
1 53 "	8 52 "	" Doyle "	271	7 50 "	11 02 "
2 30 "	9 06 "	" Parlins "	279	7 35 "	10 29 "
3 48 "	9 36 "	" Gunnison "	290	7 10 "	9 35 "
4 45 "	10 05 "	" Kezar "	302	6 42 "	8 10 "
5 25 "	10 23 "	" Cebolla "	309	6 25 "	7 37 "
6 05 "	10 43 "	" Sapinero "	316	6 05 "	7 03 "
6 50 "	11 08 "	" Currecanti "	323	5 45 "	6 30 "
7 30 "	11 31 "	" Crystal Creek "	329	5 23 "	5 55 "
*7 41 " 8 00 "	*11 38 " 11 58 "	Ar./Lv. Cimarron Lv./Ar.	331	5 15 " 5 13 "	5 45 " *5 30 "
8 40 "	12 33 p.m.	" Cerro Lv.	336	4 50 "	4 50 "
9 25 "	1 03 "	" Cedar Creek "	343	4 16 "	3 55 "
10 25 "	1 30 "	" Montrose "	353	3 45 "	3 00 "
11 40 "	1 52 "	" Colorow "	364	3 15 "	1 52 "
1 00 p.m.	2 15 "	" Delta "	375	2 48 "	1 00 p.m.
2 05 "	2 51 "	" Escalanti "	387	2 12 "	11 50 a.m.
2 37 "	3 08 "	" Dominguez "	392	1 54 "	11 15 "
3 03 "	3 29 "	" Bridgeport "	399	1 23 "	10 35 "
3 55 "	3 55 "	" Kahnah "	409	1 02 "	9 35 "
4 14 "	4 04 "	" White Water "	412	12 51 "	9 16 "
*6 15 "	4 45 "	" Grand Junction "	425	12 10 a.m.	*8 00 "
6 55 "	5 01 "	" Roan "	433	11 47 p.m.	6 44 "
7 35 p.m.	5 15 p.m.	Lv. Fruitvale Lv.	439	11 35 p.m.	6 10 a.m.

Denver and Rio Grande Railway

DENVER AND OGDEN LINE.—Continued.

Westward: No 49. Emigrant.	Westward: Pacific Express.	Stations.	Miles.	Eastward: Atlantic Express.	Eastward: No. 10. Emigrant.
7 40 p.m.	5 31 p.m.	Lv. Crevasse Lv.	446	11 20 p.m.	5 35 a.m.
8 08 "	5 44 "	" Shale "	452	11 05 "	5 05 "
8 40 "	5 55 "	" Excelsior "	457	10 54 "	4 40 "
9 15 "	6 08 "	" Acheron "	463	10 38 "	4 02 "
10 12 "	6 32 "	" West Water "	474	10 12 "	3 00 "
10 45 "	6 45 "	" Cottonwood "	479	9 57 "	2 28 "
11 55 "	7 08 "	" Cisco "	490	9 32 "	1 25 a.m.
1 23 a.m.	7 45 "	" Sagers "	507	8 50 "	11 55 p.m.
2 10 "	8 02 "	" Thompson's "	515	8 30 "	11 00 "
2 39 "	8 15 "	" Crescent "	521	8 15 "	10 22 "
3 17 "	8 30 "	" Little Grand "	529	7 57 "	9 33 "
3 55 "	8 45 "	" Solitude "	537	7 40 "	8 45 "
5 15 "	9 15 "	" Green River "	545	7 20 "	7 20 "
6 30 "	9 45 "	" Desert "	558	6 50 "	5 30 "
7 45 " *8 00 "	9 55 " *10 15 "	Ar./Lv. Lower Price Cros'. Lv./Ar.	570	*6 25 " 6 10 "	3 45 " ....
9 00 "	10 43 "	" Grassy Trail Lv.	582	5 44 "	2 37 "
9 45 "	11 07 "	" Sunny Side "	591	5 22 "	1 44 "
10 35 "	11 30 "	" Farnham "	600	5 00 "	12 48 p.m.
1 05 p.m.	12 40 a.m.	" Castle Gate "	624	4 00 "	10 25 a.m.
*3 55 "	1 35 "	" Pleasant Valley Junc. "	627	3 20 "	9 10 "
4 30 "	1 55 "	" Soldier Summit "	644	2 55 "	7 45 "
5 20 "	2 35 "	" Clear Creek "	651	2 15 "	6 45 "
6 10 "	2 57 "	" Mill Fork "	658	1 55 "	6 00 "
7 10 "	3 30 "	" Thistle "	669	1 25 "	5 00 "
8 05 "	4 00 "	" Spanish Fork "	680	12 55 "	4 00 "
8 35 "	4 10 "	" Springville "	684	12 45 "	3 20 "
.... 9 15 "	4 21 " 4 23 "	Ar./Lv. Provo Lv./Ar.	689	12 30 " *12 10 p.m.	2 30 " ....
10 00 "	4 46 "	" Battle Creek Lv.	699	11 51 a.m.	1 30 "
10 17 "	4 55 "	" American Fork "	702	11 43 "	1 09 "
10 35 "	5 03 "	" Lehi "	705	11 35 "	12 45 a.m.
11 45 "	5 40 "	" Draper "	718	11 05 "	11 45 p.m.
12 20 a.m.	5 54 "	" Bingham Junction "	724	10 52 "	11 09 "
1 15 " 1 50 "	6 20 " 6 30 "	Ar./Lv. Salt Lake Lv./Ar.	735	10 30 " 10 20 "	10 00 " 9 30 "
2 35 "	6 51 "	" Wood Cross Lv.	743	10 03 "	8 41 "
3 12 "	7 07 "	" Farmington "	750	9 50 "	8 05 "
3 32 "	7 15 "	" Kaysville "	754	9 43 "	7 45 "
4 26 "	7 40 "	" Hooper "	764	9 23 "	6 47 "
5 00 a.m.	7 55 a.m.	Ar. Ogden Lv.	771	9 10 a.m.	6 10 p.m.

Passengers holding Second-Class tickets are carried in handsome Coaches attached to Express Trains. At present Third-Class through Passengers are also transported on Express Trains in Free Emigrant Sleepers.

Ogden, Bingham and Springville Local Trains.

Northward: Bingham Passenger.	Northward: Springville Passenger.	Stations.	Miles.	Southward: Springville Passenger.	Southward: Bingham Passenger.
....	7 25 a.m.	Lv. Springville Ar.	87	7 20 p.m.	....
....	7 39 "	" Provo Lv.	82	7 06 "	....
....	8 02 "	" Battle Creek "	73	6 43 "	....
....	8 10 "	" American Fork "	69	6 33 "	....
....	8 20 "	" Lehi "	66	6 25 "	....
....	8 51 "	" Draper "	53	5 52 "	....
2 30 p.m.	....	" Bingham Ar.	63	....	9 10 a.m.
3 30 "	9 07 "	" Bingham Junction Lv.	47	5 35 "	7 55 "
4 00 " 4 10 "	9 35 " 9 40 "	Ar./Lv. Salt Lake Lv./Ar.	36	5 10 " 5 00 "	7 25 " 8 00 p.m.
4 35 "	10 03 "	" Woods Cross Lv.	28	4 35 "	7 40 "
4 51 "	10 22 "	" Farmington "	22	4 18 "	7 22 "
5 00 "	10 31 "	" Kaysville "	17	4 10 "	7 13 "
5 25 "	10 59 "	" Hooper "	7	3 45 "	6 47 "
5 40 p.m.	11 15 a.m.	Ar. Ogden Lv.	..	3 30 p.m.	6 30 p.m

SAN LUIS BRANCH.

Southward	Southward: Passenger.	Stations.	Miles.	Northward: Passenger.	Northward
....	7 15 p.m.	Lv. Denver Ar.	......	7 10 a.m.	....
....	12 55 a.m.	" South Pueblo "	120	1 55 "	....
....	7 30 "	" Salida "	217	5 35 p.m.	....
....	8 55 "	" Mears "	223	4 20 "	....
....	9 22 "	" Poncha Pass Lv.	231	3 50 "	....
....	9 47 "	" Round Hill "	234	3 25 "	....
....	11 10 "	" Villa Grove "	247	2 20 "	....
....	12 10 p.m.	Ar. Hot Springs Lv.	255	12 50 p.m.	....

Helper was not noted on this Denver and Rio Grande Railway timetable from January 15, 1884. Passengers were afforded a brief 15 to 20 minute stopover at Lower Price Crossing, 35 miles south of Price, and another one at Provo. The entire trip from Denver, Colorado, to Ogden, Utah, on either the *Pacific* or *Atlantic Express*, took 36 hours. However, if one was traveling on the east or westbound *Emigrant*, the 771-mile trip took a leisurely 80 hours to complete. The notation at the bottom of the table states, "Passengers holding Second-class tickets are carried in handsome coaches attached to Express Trains. At present Third-class through Passengers are also transported on Express Trains in Free Emigrant Sleepers."

By 1890, Helper was beginning to blossom into a full-fledged community. The town even acquired its first post office, which was housed in small wooden frame building near the depot on Main Street. James W. Miller, the postmaster, accepted his commission on December 9, 1896. Note the two children in the window and the man's head at the door peering at the photographer.

Everything in Helper was located near the railroad tracks. This 1890 photograph shows the students of Miss Parrot (back row, far left) at the Helper School. The school was located in a wood-framed house just south of the railroad yards and the roundhouse. Five of Teancum Pratt's sons—Lehi, Joseph, Moroni, Parley, and Nephi—are pictured (back row, starting fourth from the left).

When the railroad came to town, so did the businesses. Helper's business district began to grow and attract entrepreneurs who opened up saloons, pool halls, and boardinghouses. This photograph from 1900 shows the standard "boom town" style wooden buildings that lined early Helper's Main Street. The building (second from right) next to B. F. Moss's Barber Shop and Furnished Rooms is a Greek establishment with a pool hall and ice-cream parlor.

Directly behind the railroad hotel, more permanent buildings were constructed. This early photograph, *c.* 1910, shows a meat market, bakery, grocery store, notions, and dry goods store. Stores like this one were not only beneficial to the townspeople, but also to the travelers who stayed at the nearby hotel or had a few minutes before their trains departed.

18

Rio Grande Western Engine No. 144 waits with her engineer and fireman in the south Helper rail yard *c.* 1890. The engine is a Class C-26 2-8-0 made by Baldwin. It had 140 pounds of boiler pressure and 25,600 pounds of tractive effort on 51-inch drivers. The engine was renumbered to No. 663 and dismantled in August 1924.

Rio Grande Western Engine No. 70 sits on the turntable in 1890. No. 70 was a Class T-19 4-6-0 built by Baldwin. The engine weighed 134,000 pounds with 18,666 pounds of tractive effort on 67-inch drivers. It was rebuilt to standard gauge in 1898 and renumbered 715. The Denver and Rio Grande Western renumbered the engine again to No. 526; it was dismantled in August 1924.

An eastbound passenger train led by Rio Grande Western No. 302 pauses for a photograph in the east end of the Helper yard c. 1900. No. 302 was a Class C-38 2-8-0 built by Richmond in 1900. The engine weighed 183,000 pounds and had 38,054 pounds of tractive effort on 56-inch drivers. No. 302 was renumbered twice, to Nos. 962 and 902, and was dismantled in May 1936.

By the late 1890s, Helper's railroad yards dominated the landscape. Looking to the north in this photograph around 1892, the siding appears to be storage for the caboose and the roundhouse is visible on the right. The new steam electric plant was located near the roundhouse and provided light for the railroad yards. The town's face was changed forever with the coming of the 1900s.

Two

"Helper, Utah, America"

Once the railroad had established itself in Helper, the call went out for workers to populate the town. The Denver and Rio Grande actively recruited its labor force from overseas. These immigrants, driven by natural disasters and political crises in their homelands, flocked to eastern Utah looking for a better way of life.

Helper, Utah, became a destination, a reference point in America, like New York City or Chicago. The only English that most of the newcomers could speak was the phrase "Helper, Utah, America." With those three words, the immigration officials would be able to send them in the proper direction to their new home.

They brought with them their cultures, which soon infused the shops and businesses that lined Helper's Main Street. Japanese noodle houses stood next to Greek coffee shops. The sweet smell of Italian and Greek bread baking in large outdoor ovens mixed with the strong smells of the Asian fish market. American movies played upstairs at the theater, while in the basement, Japanese Kabuki entertained the crowds. Walking down the bustling street, one could count 27 different languages being spoken.

Upon settling in Helper, the settlers quickly made themselves at home. One immigrant from southern Italy expressed his frustration with the rest of America when he recounted a story of a trip back east. Upon picking up arriving family members, the immigrant told his family that he had "had enough of these United States! I want to go back to Helper, Utah!"

The perfect example of Helper's railroad labor, Japanese railroad worker Tomojiro Asahara poses in front of Engine No. 190. Asahara immigrated to Helper in the early 1920s and lived next to the steam power plant in the Helper rail yard. His tent featured an American flag and a hand-lettered sign in Japanese that read, "Tomojiro Asahara Photographer." Asahara took hundreds of photographs of the area when he was not working on the Rio Grande. When the Depression rocked the country in the 1930s, Asahara returned to his native Japan and never came back to Helper. He used the money he made while in Helper to build an "American" style home in Japan that is still in his family.

Italians quickly became the largest of the immigrant groups to move to Helper. Many tried their hands at coal mining or railroading and decided that the lifestyle was not for them. Here the New York Store, a general store advertising fruits, candy, cigars, and provisions, was built on Helper's Main Street, owned and operated by Italian immigrants August Santoline, Grosso Guariente, and Eugene Guariente.

The Italians began their own band in Helper. They played at dances, ball games, and of course funerals. The 18 members and some onlookers pose for a photograph in 1914 with the Helper depot in the background. Italian bands always contained at least one accordion player and oftentimes a bagpiper. While not as well known as Scottish bagpipes, Italian bagpipes were quite common.

After the Italians, the Greeks were the largest immigrant group in Helper. Like other immigrant groups, the Greeks were segregated in Helper and in the surrounding mining camps. "Greek Towns," as they were often called, had large outdoor ovens where bread was baked daily. In this 1910 photograph, these Greek men gathered for some socializing after a hard day's work.

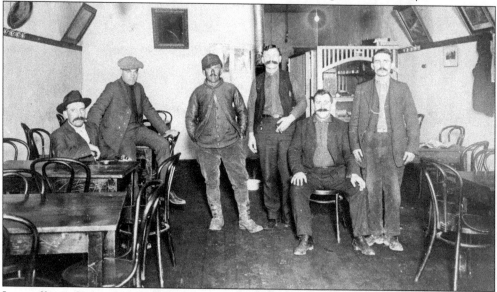

In an effort to better accommodate the growing immigrant population of Helper, ethnic-specific businesses began to spring up on Main Street, such as this Greek coffeehouse, seen around 1920. The coffeehouses were "men only" establishments where alcohol flowed freely and Greek pipes and some friendly gambling were abundant. These places offered the immigrants a taste of home and allowed them precious time away from work.

In the early 1900s, Helper began to take shape as a bustling railroad center. This photograph, taken c. 1906 looking south from the top of Balanced Rock Mountain, shows the town spreading out to fill the valley below. The busy railroad yards with the roundhouse and the maintenance shack are visible at the center left of the photograph, while the Price River is visible on the right.

Helper's distinct character came from the immigrants who called it home. This c. 1907 photograph shows the newly completed, hand-carved, brick Barboglio Building, constructed by Italian immigrant and labor organizer Joseph Barboglio right next to the rock Lowenstein Building, erected by a Jewish merchant. The saloon was owned by Celeste Dalpiaz. The covered wagon and the dirt street add an unmistakable western flavor.

By the 1900s, Helper had already earned the reputation for having more bars and brothels than churches, a reputation that it held until recent years. The central part of Main Street featured one bar after another, such as the Zang Bar and the Flaim Saloon, pictured here in 1909. The unnamed bar next to the Flaim Saloon proudly advertises Becker's beer and Crystal Brook whiskey. At one time, 27 different bars serviced the community. On the weekends and on paydays, the town's population tripled in size with men from the railroad and surrounding mining camps making their way into town with full pockets, and stumbling out with empty ones. This wild-and-wooly atmosphere made Helper the black sheep of Utah.

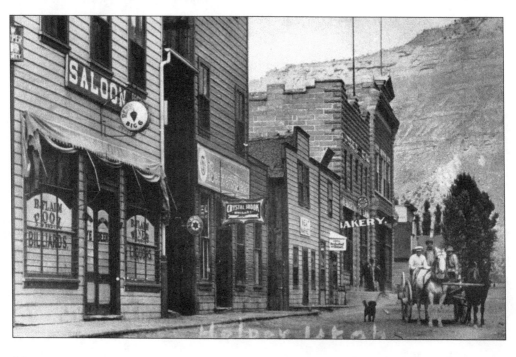

The D&R.G.Depot, Helper, Utah.

Changes were happening at the railroad as well as in town. By 1900, the Denver and Rio Grande Western Railroad had built a new depot in Helper. This depot was more stylish than the previous one and featured reading rooms, men and women's waiting rooms, and a larger loading dock. In this *c.* 1906 photograph, the fine Victorian touches on the building are evident.

"HELPER UTAH"

This *c.* 1910 photograph postcard shows the new depot and bustling rail yards. A loaded coal train waits for helper engines to be attached while men rush to wait for the next passenger express. This scene greeted arriving immigrants as they ended their long journey in their new home.

In 1905, the railroad undertook a new construction project in Helper with the building of the three-story Young Men's Christian Association (YMCA) building. Completed in February 1906, the YMCA was a gem amongst the Helper rail yards. Used by railroad workers and the community alike, the YMCA offered space for school classes and activities for the town's children. The first secretary was Julius Sheppard, who retired in 1926.

Located near the depot, the Helper YMCA provided a welcoming sight to travelers arriving in town. Many were surprised to see such lavish buildings so well appointed. By April 1906, membership in the organization was 328 men, with the rooms being filled day and night. Members were charged the modest fee of 15¢ for 12 hours of occupation.

In addition to the popular reading room and library at the Helper YMCA, the organization offered a wide variety of activities. Bowling alleys were busy in the basement of the building, and gymnasium classes were taught six days a week. The YMCA even purchased land and organized its own baseball team. Men's meetings were held every Sunday. The Helper YMCA, built by gifts of $25,000 each from Gen. William J. Palmer and George Foster Peabody, was the first of two YMCAs built for the Denver and Rio Grande Railroad. The Helper Association was one of 246 organizations located at railroad division points across North America. According to a promotional booklet written by Edwin L. Hamilton for the Helper YMCA, the reason for the existence of the building was summed up simply: "It works."

The ethnic diversity of the Denver and Rio Grande Western's labor force is evident in this c. 1910 photograph taken in the Helper rail yard. Japanese, Irish, Italian, Greek, Yugoslavian, Scottish, Basque, and Hispanic immigrants worked together to make the railroad a power force through the mountains. Even though they were from diverse backgrounds, they mostly put aside their differences, worked as a team, and created a culturally unique home in Utah.

With scores of trains passing through Helper every day, the roundhouse was a busy place. This c. 1910 photograph shows the car man and maintenance departments. The engines and cars were kept in top operating shape by this group of mechanics.

An eastbound train pulled by Engine No. 1145 stops for a unique photograph in front of the railroad hotel. Engine No. 1145 was a Class C-48 2-8-0 engine built by Schenectady. Originally built with 42,000 pounds of tractive effort, the series was rebuilt to 48,000 pounds when superheated and 44,000 pounds normally with an increased engine weight of 220,440 pounds. This engine was dismantled in 1946.

Denver and Rio Grande Engine No. 770 sits proudly on the turntable at the Helper roundhouse surrounded by her crew and the roundhouse workers c. 1910. D&RG No. 770 was a Class T-29 4-6-0 built by Brooks. The engine weighed in at 184,000 pounds with 29,093 pounds of tractive effort on 67-inch drivers. Built in 1908, the engine was dismantled in January 1939.

By 1900, the railroad had completed 20 cottages for its employees. The five- or six-room cottages were equipped with water inside and out, electric lights supplied by the railroad's own steam plant, and landscaping. All of this was available to the railroad worker and his family for a mere $1 per month for each room. This photograph, c. 1905, shows a neat row of nine cottages next to the rail yard.

At the beginning of the 20th century, Helper, along with other towns in the area, established its own school district and board of trustees. The Helper Central School, located on the south end of town near the tracks, held classes for elementary and junior high school students, while high school students attended classes 6 miles south in Price. This 1906 photograph postcard shows the school shortly after it opened.

This c. 1910 view of Helper, taken from the western hilltop, shows how much the town had begun to grow. The newly constructed Helper Central School is at center, and the large YMCA building is next to the tracks. The railroad's employee housing is visible on the left while an early canal (far left) feeds one of the large working farms in the town.

A closer view of downtown, c. 1910, shows from left to right the railroad chapel, the depot, the beanery, and the YMCA. Employee cottages were located behind the depot building and along Main Street. This postcard, published by A. J. Stafford, used the top of the Lowenstein Mercantile to identify the town as "Helper, Utah."

The prosperity that the railroad brings was evidenced in 1914 when Joseph Barboglio (center left) opened the Helper State Bank. The bank building used the upstairs space for doctors and professional offices. The bank was located next to the A. D. Sutton Drug Company and the Tokyo Restaurant. By 1920, Barboglio operated two separate banks, one in Helper and one in Price.

The attractive front yard of the railroad hotel was a wonderful sight for weary travelers. It was a first-class hotel with a lush lawn and towering poplar trees. The hotel offered both overnight guests and railroad travelers a hot meal for either lunch or dinner. This postcard sent from Helper to Galax, Virginia, on September 19, 1910 shows Helper as a civilized location worthy of a visit. (Courtesy SueAnn Martell.)

Travelers soon began to enjoy all that Helper had to offer. This group posed for a photograph in the Price River on their way to catch a train in October 1908. According to the note on the back, they were leaving town after visiting the woman's brother, who lived in Helper. The notation on the front of the photograph draws attention to the "graceful position of Jeannette" in the river. (Courtesy SueAnn Martell.)

Around 1916, Helper's city hall (right) was located in a small, wooden building on Main Street. Although moved from its original location, the building is still used on Main Street and is one of the oldest buildings in town. The Lowenstein Mercantile (left center) is also still in use, having been restored. Unfortunately the Golden Rule Store and the neighboring Barboglio building were destroyed in a fire in 1950.

Helper's Liberty Theater, c. 1910, was a hotbed of entertainment. The theater featured a roll-up dance floor that was removed for sporting events. World-famous boxer Jack Dempsey trained in Helper and challenged local men to friendly fights at the Liberty. In 1923, the *Ogden Standard Examiner* reported that Dempsey was "holding heavy workouts at Helper in preparation for his match against Tom Gibbons." Dempsey received $300,000 for the fight.

There was nothing like an afternoon baseball game to relieve the tensions of daily life. Here a group of men and boys gathered near the railroad tracks on the YMCA baseball field c. 1912. Baseball was as much a social affair as it was an athletic event. Everyone dressed in their Sunday best to attend the competitions. All of the towns had their own baseball teams and competed throughout the state.

On Sunday, June 24, 1917, the Mammoth Reservoir, or Gooseberry Dam, 20 miles west of Scofield, Utah, broke, sending a wall of water down the canyon. The break was reported to the Denver and Rio Grande Western Railroad about 2:00 p.m., and officials were urged to plan for the devastation. Despite their efforts, the cost to the railroad was reported at nearly $1 million, with nearly equal losses reported by the coal mines that depended on the railroad for the transportation of their coal. Eight steel bridges were lost. Railroad officials suspended all operations west of Helper, estimating that at least 20 miles of track would have to be rebuilt. In the town of Castle Gate, three miles northwest of Helper, the disaster claimed numerous residences and even the Castle Gate depot.

The Denver and Rio Grande Western was completely shut down west of Helper for over 10 days. Several freight trains full of coal and at least two Mallet engines were marooned between Colton and Helper. One thousand men from the surrounding mining camps came to the aid of the railroad to assist with the reconstruction. However, with all of the damage, only one person—Hattie Peacock—lost her life after traveling down to the river to watch the flood. Although the railroad was reopened within a short amount of time, the cleanup took many weeks. Crews were faced with removing over 6 feet of debris in some locations.

An unidentified steam engine leaves the Helper roundhouse c. 1917. After the Gooseberry flood was cleaned up, it was business as usual for the Helper division point. Coal began moving more quickly through Helper as the mines tried to catch up with their contracts; they were completely shut down during the disaster. That shutdown also resulted in a loss for the smelting companies in the East.

The crew of an unidentified 2-8-0 engine poses while she blows off some steam in the Helper rail yard on a winter's day c. 1915. This engine was probably going to be pressed into helper service for the climb to Soldier Summit. The toughest part of the climb for westbound trains was from Castle Gate to the tunnel at Kyune.

Denver and Rio Grande Western Engine No. 1057 pulled out of the Helper roundhouse for a portrait with the entire work crew and Helper officials *c.* 1911. No. 1057 was a Class L-62 2-6-6-2 Schenectady 1910. This monster weighed 340,000 pounds, had 62,026 pounds of tractive effort with 57-inch drivers, and carried 200 pounds of boiler pressure. The engine was renumbered to

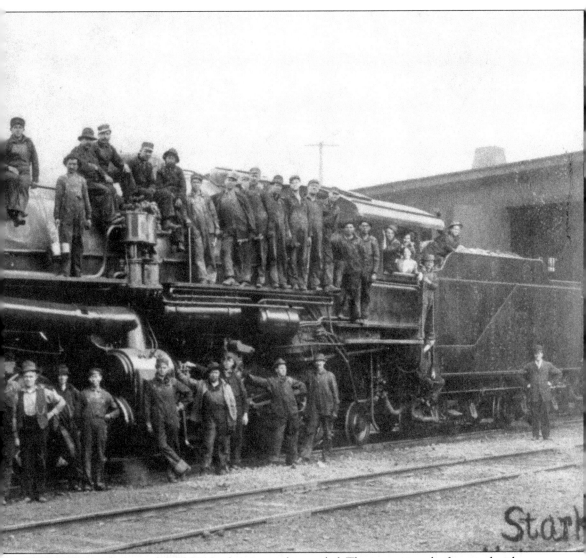

Stark

3307 in 1924 and was used until 1946, when it was dismantled. The woman on the front end with the hat and necktie was the maintenance department secretary; the identity of the woman in the cab is unknown. The photograph was taken by a local Helper photographer named Stark. All in all, 44 people flanked No. 1057 for her portrait—a lot of people for a very large engine.

Two former Rio Grande Western engines head up a westbound passenger train near the Helper boardinghouse. The lead engine, No. 955, was a Class G-28 2-6-0 Schenectady 1901 weighing 154,400 pounds with 27,535 pounds of tractive effort on 61-inch drivers and 190 pounds of boiler pressure. Operating on the Rio Grande Western, No. 955 was numbered 505. It was renumbered 595 in 1924 and dismantled in January 1937. The second engine was a Class T-24 4-6-0, also built by Schenectady in 1901. This was the larger of the two engines, weighing 161,500 pounds with 67-inch drivers. Although larger, the second engine had less tractive effort—24,400 pounds—and carried 185 pounds of boiler pressure. (Courtesy SueAnn Martell.)

Three

Black Diamonds on Steel Rails

For over 28 years, the Denver and Rio Grande Western Railroad had been the dominant force in eastern Utah railroading. It controlled the passenger and freight traffic. A dispute had arisen between the coal producers and the railroad over the D&RGW's ability to move all of the coal mined throughout the region in a timely fashion. United States Smelting, Refining, and Mining Company took notice, and in 1911, a new railroad came to the table.

In an effort to protect its interests in the Utah coalfields, United States Smelting, Refining, and Mining Company issued a statement saying, "It's wholly apparent that existing railroad faculties could not render competent service." With that statement, the Utah Railway Company was incorporated in 1912.

Worried by this new competition, the Denver and Rio Grande Western quickly offered an olive branch. They would complete improvements to their line, double track the route, and offer Utah Railway trackage rights if the Utah Railway would reciprocate and offer the same deal on their newly completed line from Thistle to Provo. After many negotiations, the final agreement was signed in 1913 for a jointly operated, double-track system that still exists.

Today the Utah Railway provides local mines with coal service, which makes up approximately 95 percent of its business. The Utah was purchased by Genesee and Wyoming in 2002 and maintains 98 miles of its own track, part of which is the original Utah Railway Junction–Mohrland line, and 205 miles of trackage rights, including the jointly operated system with Union Pacific.

Starting its life as a scrappy little short line, the Utah Railway ended up moving millions of tons of black diamonds efficiently on steel rails.

After beginning its life as the Utah Coal Route in 1911, the new railroad in town soon changed its name in incorporation papers to the Utah Coal Railway Company on January 24, 1912. In this c. 1940 photograph, a Utah Railway Company open gondola car, No. 217, sits loaded at the Martin rail yards.

The main purpose of the Utah Railway Company was to provide the shortest route between Provo, Utah, and its coal interests. To meet that goal, the main line between the Utah Railway Junction at Martin and the new coal camp of Mohrland was completed. In this 1912 photograph, a Utah Railway 2-8-0 Lima waits near Mohrland. Utah Railway had three Limas in its roster, all purchased from other routes.

Construction of the Utah Railway Junction–Mohrland line was completed on October 31, 1914, a little over two years from the date it was started. Seen in this *c.* 1940 photograph is the east portal of Tunnel No. 2. Construction also included a cutoff line for the Castle Valley Railway, known as the Black Hawk–Mohrland. The Utah Railway Company purchased this cutoff at a cost of $246,911.

The crowning gem of the 25.78-mile Utah Railway Junction–Mohrland line is the Gordon Creek Bridge. Standing 135 feet tall and spanning 634 feet, it is the longest steel girder bridge of its kind in Utah. As the bridge reached completion, construction crews received help placing the heavy ties from a Utah Railway Company crane.

The construction of the Utah Railway Junction–Mohrland line was funded with short-term notes backed by the United States Smelting, Refining, and Mining Company. When completed, the cost of the line was $3,383,510. This photograph of the bridge shows a section of the rail in place. The Utah Railway Company used date nails, which are spikes with the date fired into the tops, to identify when the rails and the ties had been laid down.

Construction of the bridge was delayed when the conditions of the soil forced the bridge to be lengthened and a flash flood swept away the construction materials. Still in use today, the Gordon Creek Bridge, built at a 60-degree curve, is a sight to be seen. This c. 1940 photograph was taken looking south towards Mohrland.

In 1927, the Utah Railway Company expanded its rail yards at Martin and constructed a two-story brick office building on a hill above the engine house. This *c.* 1928 photograph shows the new office building and one of their large Baldwin locomotives. By 1918, the Utah owned 16 locomotives for its Utah Railway Junction–Mohrland line.

After a fire destroyed the original engine house at Martin, the structure was rebuilt in 1922. In this *c.* 1923 photograph, Engine Nos. 4, 103, and 202 receive service at Martin. Engine No. 4 was a 2-8-0 Alco-Schenectady built in 1910, No. 103 was a 2-10-2 Baldwin built in 1917, and No. 202 was a 2-8-8-0 Baldwin built in 1918.

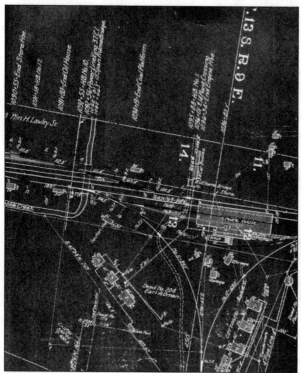

Drawn in 1927, this abstract of the rail yard at Martin shows the expansion of the Utah Railway operations from September 7, 1912, to August 1924. The abstract looks west toward the office building and the engine house. Cottages and apartments built for employees are visible at the lower right of the diagram. (Courtesy SueAnn Martell.)

While the Utah Railway Junction–Mohrland line was secured, the problem of getting the coal over Soldier Summit needed to be solved. The Utah Railway proposed a route similar to that of the Denver and Rio Grande Western. In 1913, a trackage agreement was signed by the two parties that is still in effect today. Pictured here around 1914, a section crew under foreman Joe Bonacci works on the double track near Thistle.

Engine No. 102 poses for a photograph on the Utah Railway line near Mohrland. No. 102 was a 2-10-2 built by Baldwin in October 1917. The Utah obtained the engine on November 28, 1917. No. 102 had 70,450 pounds of tractive effort and 63-inch drivers, and was one of six engines ordered by the Utah in December 1916. The engine was scrapped in March 1957.

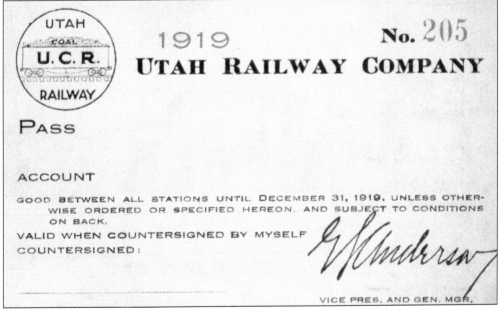

This unissued Utah Railway Company pass from 1919 shows the Utah Railway's commitment to coal by still identifying themselves as the Utah Coal Route (UCR). The Utah operated six-day-a-week service for freight, mail, express, and passengers between Utah Railway Junction and Mohrland, not including mine runs. Passengers could disembark at any one of nine stations along the line.

A sore spot between United States Fuel and the Denver and Rio Grande Western was the D&RGW's mishandling of the new Utah Railway line. Complaints were flooding in that it could not keep up with demand for cars and that loaded trains sat for days waiting for locomotives. Scenes such as this one around 1916 at Black Hawk were common. Finally, on November 1, 1917, the Utah Railway took over the operation of its own trains.

The town of Hiawatha, incorporated in September 1911, was located west of the existing town of Black Hawk. In 1915, the two towns combined post offices and consolidated themselves under the Hiawatha name. This c. 1919 photograph shows the passenger and freight depot at Hiawatha. The depot, listed as "Kingmine"—which was the railroad's name for the town—was in use until 1926, when passenger service was discontinued.

A passenger train headed to Price unloads passengers at the Hiawatha depot *c. 1920*. In the background, the tipple for the Hiawatha mine stands ready for the next shift. The tipple is a large building where coal is deposited from the small mine cars (upper right of the tipple), sorted, and loaded into railcars for transportation. In 1930 alone, the Utah Railway hauled 1,569,777 tons of coal and 10,538 tons of miscellaneous materials.

The neat coal camp of Hiawatha is bordered by the Utah Railway yards in this *c. 1920* photograph. The open-topped steel gondola cars are loaded with coal awaiting transport. By 1918, the three mines owned by the United States Fuel Company—Hiawatha, Black Hawk, and Mohrland—were producing 6,000 tons of coal per day, and the Utah was shipping 30,000 tons per week.

Coal dust and steam engine smoke fill the sky over Hiawatha on December 22, 1934. The Depression hit the Utah Railway hard, as coal mines began to shut down and towns began to dwindle. Through the 1930s, Hiawatha remained an active coal mine, mechanizing its mining operations and eventually consolidating the King No. 1 mine at Hiawatha with the King No. 2 mine at Mohrland.

A double lash-up of steam engines chugs up the grade between Utah Railway Junction and Hiawatha. The lead engine is Utah Railway No. 3, an ex–Castle Valley Railroad 2-8-0 Lima built in 1912. The Utah Railway leased No. 3 from December 1, 1917, until it was purchased by the Utah on July 1, 1918. The second engine appears to be another Lima 2-8-0.

July 27th 1914

In eastern Utah, the railroads and coal mines are inextricably linked. This July 27, 1914, photograph, taken at Hiawatha, shows the instruction and rescue car for the Black Hawk, Castle Valley, Consolidated Fuel, and Castle Gate Coal companies. The passenger railcar had been retrofitted for mobile training of mine rescue workers and for use as a command center during mine disasters.

The mine in Mohrland was a considerable distance away from the Utah Railway yards. Here lump coal is removed from the mine with a locomotive and driven down the canyon to the tipple at the rail yard c. 1925. The Hiawatha-Mohrland area was considered to have the best coal and the best mining conditions of any of the coalfields in the Wasatch Plateau.

UTAH RAILWAY COMPANY

CHARGE TO 308-BS

M-ORDER NO. 121

DATE Provo, Ut., Sept. 19, 1947

(3) TO Mr. W. E. Berrey, Dist Foreman

Provo

RECEIVED

SEP 2 0 1947

UTAH RAILWAY COMPANY

SALT LAKE CITY, UTAH

DETAIL OF PERFORMANCE

Make repairs to Locomotive 107: Class 3.

(This locomotive has made 33,147 miles between Class 5 in
July 1946 and August 31, 1947. Total miles made to date
of this shopping will be furnished as soon as available.)

CC- GSA JLD RSK TW

General Foreman will report promptly the completion, alteration, or cancellation of work. Care should be exercised by
supervisory forces to instruct all men engaged in the performance to charge labor and material to this order. Daily time slips
of employes should be inspected carefully to insure correct charge to this order, and before approving time slip.

L. R. TAYLOR

MASTER MECHANIC

Repairs were ordered to Utah Railway Engine No. 107, a Baldwin 2-10-2 built in October 1920, on September 19, 1947. No. 107 had logged 33,147 miles between July 1946 and August 1947. In 1931, repairs of Utah engines were no longer being made at the shops in Martin but in Provo, Utah. No. 107 served the Utah several more years before being scrapped in September 1954.

In February 1913, the United States Fuel Company had orders for 1,400 cars of coal that were never filled due to a lack of coal cars. In this 1947 photograph, a steel 50-ton gondola car awaits loading. The car is marked UCR, or Utah Coal Route. The Utah Coal Route marking became a marketing tool for 2,000 coal cars owned jointly by the Utah Railway and the Los Angeles and Salt Lake.

In another disagreement with the Denver and Rio Grande Western, the mining companies of Peerless, Spring Canyon, and Standardville organized the Utah Terminal Railway in 1920. Previously served by the D&RGW, the three mines were unhappy with the larger railroad's inability to provide sufficient railcars and switching service. Paralleling the D&RGW tracks for four miles, the Utah Railway constructed the branch line from Standardville to Jacobs, where the line connected with the Utah Railway. The D&RGW protested the construction, but the state determined that the competition would do the area good. The 4.9-percent grade was easy on loaded coal trains as it was downhill all the way. This photograph shows the slack plant at the Peerless mine as a Utah Coal Route gondola car prepares for loading. Master mechanic Henry Draper is standing on the conveyer.

Another coal mine operated by the United States Fuel Company, parent company of the Utah Railway, was the Panther Mine located a half mile from the Utah Railway Junction. Like other United States Fuel mines, Panther was serviced by the Denver and Rio Grande Western until the Utah took over operations in 1917. This c. 1920 photograph of the Panther tipple shows the Utah Coal Route gondolas being loaded.

Incorporated in 1909, the Helper Western Railway was conceived to service proposed coal lands in the Gordon Creek area of the Wasatch Plateau. Construction of the route began in 1922, and the rails were laid by the Utah Railway in 1925. During construction, the name was changed to the National Coal Railway. This c. 1926 photograph shows construction crews from the Utah Railway installing a water tank at National Junction.

The sale of the National Coal Railway to the Utah Railway became final on March 11, 1926. Here Engine No. 202 and Caboose No. 54 are helping to move the massive water tower into place. The tower is situated on a jointly owned Utah Railway and Los Angeles and Salt Lake flat car. The branch line was originally proposed to leave from Helper; however, the company was unable to secure enough funds for a line of that size. The finished branch was an 8.9-mile road from National Junction on the Utah Railway to the north fork of Gordon Creek at Sweet Mine. In November 1936, the Utah Railway disassociated itself from the National Coal Railway, which had served as a subsidiary of the Utah. By the winter of 1943, the Utah Railway was moving a loaded train of coal per day out of the National Branch.

This bill of lading, dated May 20, 1932, was issued from the Sweet Coal Company. The Sweet Mine issued the paper for the consignment of one carload of slack coal to the Combined Metals Reduction Company in Bauer, Utah. The order was moved on the Utah Railway National branch with the delivering carrier being the Los Angeles and Salt Lake Railroad. According to the weigh master, the coal car was "loaded to full visible capacity."

The town of Consumers was owned and operated by the Consumers Mutual Coal Company. In November 1926, a new tipple was completed, which made it one of the most modern coal-producing plants in the country. The only one of its kind in Utah, the tipple automatically sorted the coal into five different grades with five separate tipple tracks to allow each grade to be loaded simultaneously.

Loaded coal trains line up below Consumers in 1937 with a loaded train being moved by Utah Railway Engine No. 201, a Baldwin 2-8-8-0 built in 1918. It had 57-inch drivers and 103,000 pounds of tractive effort. In 1926, Consumers Mutual Coal Company built a bridge to hold two of these giants and 60 loaded cars at a cost of about $60,000.

A confusing maze of railroad tracks and mine rails mark the boundary between the towns of National (foreground), Consumers, and Sweet (not visible to the left). The modest employee housing at National sits across the street from the more elaborate brick homes of the company officials. The new Consumers tipple is visible in the background, while the new railroad bridge built by Morrison-Knudsen is pictured at the left, c. 1930.

A group of three gondola cars sits on the railroad tracks at Sweet Mine *c.* 1937. Located at an elevation of nearly 9,000 feet, the camps of National, Consumers, and Sweet felt the brunt of harsh winters. During the 1930s, nationally renowned photographer Dorthea Lange visited the canyon and took dozens of photographs of the town's residents struggling to make ends meet in a snowed-in coal camp where tar paper shacks were commonplace.

The Utah Railway maintained its place as the premier coal hauler in Utah into the age of diesels. In 1952, the Utah Railway purchased a fleet of engines from Alco. This *c.* 1969 photograph shows the first of these engines, RSD4 No. 300, with a coal train at Soldier Summit. In 1952 and 1953, five identical 1,600-horsepower six-motor units were added to the fleet, including the second unit in this set, RSD4 No. 305. (Courtesy SueAnn Martell.)

Four

TOWNS ALONG
THE TRACKS

In the early days of railroading in the West, railroads did not have just one hometown. About every 20 miles, the thirsty locomotives needed to take on water, tired crews needed to rest, and track needed constant maintenance. On the 75 miles of track from Helper to Provo, there were several of these villages.

Three miles north of Helper, the town of Castle Gate was founded for the rich coal deposits that could be mined for the railroad's use. Established in 1887, Castle Gate was a permanent fixture in the canyon until 1974, when the homes were picked up and moved and the rest of the town leveled to make room for a coal-processing plant.

The town of Colton rested squarely at the junction of the Pleasant Valley branch line and the D&RGW main line. It grew quickly but began to fade when the engines became more reliable and technology replaced muscle. By the 1950s, the railroad had pulled up stakes, and all that remained at the Colton town site were memories.

The little town of Tucker was born of the railroad and died by it. Tucker had a life span of less than 40 years and became the victim of technology much sooner than others when the railroad bypassed the town in 1915 in an effort to shave a few degrees off the Soldier Summit climb.

The town of Thistle, which lasted longer than any other town, did not go down without a fight. Begun nearly 100 years to the day, Thistle was destroyed when a massive mud slide swept down the canyon and backed up the river in the spring of 1983. The town and the railroad were a total loss.

All of these towns have a story, and they all revolve around the railroad. These stories can be found in the remains of the towns along the tracks.

Three miles north of Helper, the town of Castle Gate was established in 1887. By 1890, the high quality of coal in the area had attracted over 150 miners and their families. The railroad's subsidiary company, Pleasant Valley Coal Company, ran the town and the mine. The Denver and Rio Grande Western built the Castle Gate depot, seen in this *c.* 1890 photograph.

The town of Castle Gate got its name from the two rock outcroppings located north of town. Resembling the stone gate of a medieval castle, the formation appeared to "open" and "close" as one traveled through. In this *c.* 1920 postcard, a freight train with a mid-train helper set has just passed through the gate on its way west to Soldier Summit. (Courtesy SueAnn Martell.)

Following the tight, winding course of the Price River, the Denver and Rio Grande Western laid its tracks right at the base of the east "gate," the larger of the two rock formations. This c. 1890 photograph shows an eastbound freight train with an unidentified locomotive headed into Castle Gate after its decent from Soldier Summit.

The town of Castle Gate was a showplace for industry. With its bustling railroad tracks and its modern coal-mining methods, Castle Gate became a model for other company towns of the day. Made of hand-cut stone, the large Wasatch Store (center) was the main focus of the town, while the company homes spread out away from the store and massive wooden tipple in this c. 1890 photograph. Newcomers to town had to live in tents at the end of the tipple (middle right). (Courtesy SueAnn Martell.)

After working at the Magnolia Hall saloon for over a month, Butch Cassidy and his partner Elza Lay stole over $8,000 from the Castle Gate payroll on April 21, 1897. The payroll was brought into town on a special train and deposited at the Pleasant Valley Coal Company office on the upper floor of the Wasatch Store, pictured here around 1890.

The Larsen family of Castle Gate took time out of their daily activities to pose for a photograph *c.* 1900. While the homes at Castle Gate were comfortable, they were owned entirely by the mining company. After working for several years and never getting ahead in the mines, some workers left to find work on the railroad.

This Denver and Rio Grande Western wrecker crew works to clean up the derailment of a boxcar on the west end of Castle Gate c. 1920. At this time, the railroad was still using wooden gondola cars marked "D&RG" to haul the coal out of Castle Gate and its sister mine at Winter Quarters.

By the mid-1920s, Castle Gate had grown into a large town with a moderately sized railroad yard to take care of D&RGW's interests in the coal mine. Most of the mineable coal was recovered from the railroad's other mine at Winter Quarters, and the focus now was squarely on Castle Gate. This photograph shows the piles of mine timbers (center) deposited next to the railroad track.

Rio Grande Western Locomotive No. 132 poses with her crew at Castle Gate c. 1895. RGW No. 132 was renumbered by the Denver and Rio Grande Western to No. 651. A Class C-26 2-8-0, the locomotive was built by Baldwin, had 25,600 pounds of tractive effort with 51-inch drivers, and weighed 120,100 pounds. The engine was dismantled in 1916.

Castle Gate has always been a striking backdrop for photographers. In this c. 1940 photograph, Denver and Rio Grande Western Locomotive No. 3700 pulls a mixed freight train beneath the Castle Gate and past a line of empty coal cars. No. 3700 was a Class L-105 Baldwin 1938 4-6-6-4 that weighed 620,000 pounds and had 105,000 pounds of tractive effort. It was dismantled in March 1956. (Courtesy SueAnn Martell.)

A double lash-up of 2-8-8-2s provided helper power for a coal train near Castle Gate *c.* 1945. The lead engine is No. 3561, a Class L-109 built by Baldwin. Built in 1919, the 526,000-pound locomotive was purchased in early 1945 by the D&RGW from the Norfolk and Western. The second helper is No. 3509, a Class L-107 built in 1923 by Richmond that weighed 534,000 pounds. (Courtesy SueAnn Martell.)

Around 1945, No. 3702 steams up out of the yard at Castle Gate with a mixed freight train for her difficult climb to Soldier Summit. D&RGW No. 3702 was a Class L-105 4-6-6-4 built by Baldwin with 105,000 pounds of tractive effort and 255 pounds of boiler pressure. In this photograph, No. 3702 shows off the new striped nose paint that became popular after World War II. (Courtesy SueAnn Martell.)

By 1954, Utah Power and Light Company had built a steam electric generating plant at the south end of Castle Gate. In this photograph, old Rio Grande switcher unit No. 41 waits on the siding while an FT unit passes by on the way to Helper. No. 41 was a 44-ton 380 switcher that was sold to Utah Power and Light Company in August 954 for use in its coal yard.

The eastbound *California Zephyr* glides around the Castle Gate with Engine No. 5771 and three B units leading the way to Helper *c.* 1969. One of the most popular trains of all time, the Rio Grande's *California Zephyr* used 7,000-horsepower (1,750 horsepower in each "A" and "B" unit) EMD F9s to handle the steep grades between Salt Lake City and Denver.

With the vertical sandstone cliff of Castle Gate standing guard, the Denver and Rio Grande Western's eastbound *California Zephyr* passes by on its way to a stop in Helper c. 1969. The famous dome car, the Silver Sky, gave passengers a breathtaking view of the mountain scenery as they passed, making the journey from California to Denver the trip of a lifetime.

Rising to a steep 2.4-percent grade from Castle Gate to the double tunnels at the siding of Kyune, Price Canyon provides the biggest challenge for railroaders on the east side of Soldier Summit. In this c. 1900 photograph, the remoteness and steepness of the canyon is evident. The construction project through the canyon was a huge undertaking.

Founded in 1882, Pleasant Valley Junction was the connecting point between the Denver and Rio Grande Western's main line and the newly constructed Scofield branch. In the mid-1890s, Pleasant Valley Junction was changed to Colton in honor of William F. Colton, a railroad official. In this c. 1885 photograph, the depot displays the name Pleasant Valley Junction, while the sign above the door identifies it as an express station.

Narrow-gauge Locomotive No. 272 poses on the turntable at Pleasant Valley Junction with her crew c. 1888. Denver and Rio Grande Western No. 272 was a 2-8-0 Class C-16 built by Baldwin and featured a diamond stack. This nimble locomotive weighed 60,000 pounds and had 16,540 pounds of tractive effort. The engine was dismantled in October 1926.

A mixed coal and freight train stopped at Pleasant Valley Junction near the water tower *c.* 1888. By this time, Pleasant Valley Junction had developed quite a long Main Street, with businesses lined up next to railroad houses. The rail yards (right) were filled with boxcars and wooden gondola coal cars as well as several cabooses.

The new depot, seen in this photograph around 1895, shows the town's new name of Colton, which became an important stop along the Denver and Rio Grande main line. Passengers disembarked for lunch or dinner, and freight moved in and out of the town on its way to larger places. The 1902 Sears catalog quoted a price of $2.25 for shipping goods to Colton; no mention was made of Helper.

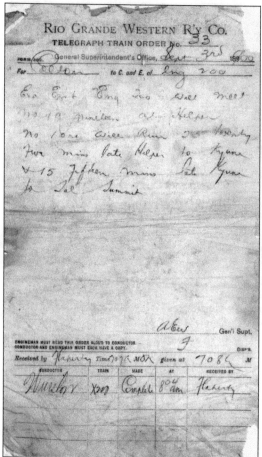

This telegraph train order was sent to Colton on September 3, 1900. The order for Engine No. 200 notifies the crew that they will meet No. 19 at Helper. It also states that No. 1 was running 25 minutes late from Helper to Kyune and 15 minutes late from Kyune to Soldier Summit. The order was telegraphed at 7:07 a.m., and the order given at 7:08 a.m.

By the early 1920s, Colton's business district had grown to include at least two hotels, the Colton and the European. The town also had a schoolhouse for their children. However, the town was slowly dying. The 1910 Census showed 194 residents, while the 1920 Census showed only 49. As technology improved and transportation became more reliable, towns like Colton were on their way to becoming ghost towns.

Colton was the scene of a horrific head-on collision on October 6, 1941. A light engine returning from helper duty was standing on the crossover, against regulations, waiting for the fireman to align all of the switches. A westbound freight called the *Flying Ute* struck No. 3593 as it came around the curve at 40 miles per hour. The *Flying Ute* was led by Engine No. 3509, a Class L-107 2-8-8-2, and Engine No. 3709, a Class L-105 4-6-6-4. Fireman J. W. Hammond was running on No. 3509 and lost his right leg below the knee in the crash. The brakeman tied his necktie on the fireman's leg to keep him from bleeding to death. Fortunately no one else was hurt or killed, and all three articulated engines were rebuilt to run again.

Originally called Clear Creek, the town site of Tucker became important in the Denver and Rio Grande's domination of the eastern Utah coalfields. It was at Tucker that the original Utah and Pleasant Valley Railroad branched off to reach the coal deposits at Winter Quarters. This line was also called "Calico Road," as the U&PV paid its employees with cloth instead of cash. This *c.* 1890 photograph shows the small depot at Tucker.

The Denver and Rio Grande began construction of the narrow-gauge main line from Helper to Provo in 1883. Construction crews created a daunting 4-percent grade from Tucker to Soldier Summit. Here the crew pauses for a photograph just outside of Tucker. Shortly after the town began, the name was changed from Clear Creek to Tucker, presumably to avoid confusion with a new coal camp in Carbon County.

Tucker boasted a three-stall engine house in its multitracked rail yard. Here Rio Grande Western Locomotive No. 147 and two of her sister engines lined up for a photograph *c.* 1892. A Class C-26 2-8-0 built by Baldwin in 1891, No. 147 had 25,600 pounds of tractive effort and weighed 120,100 pounds with 51-inch drivers. It was renumbered to No. 666 and dismantled in 1924.

Tucker grew steadily from the late 1870s through the early 1900s, reaching a peak population of approximately 500 residents. This *c.* 1882 photograph shows the main part of town (right) and the former Utah and Pleasant Valley Railroad spur heading up the canyon behind the engine house (top right). Tucker's small business district had several hotels, a few saloons, and one or two general merchants.

The railroad built an impressive schoolhouse for the children of Tucker around 1899. The school, an exact duplicate of the school that the railroad built at Thistle, sat on the old railroad grade from the Utah and Pleasant Valley line. Pictured here are 13 students playing outside of the building.

This bird's-eye view of Tucker shows the tight grouping of rail yards, a branch line, houses, farms, and a business district in the narrow canyon c. 1882. The rail yards were busy, and the Utah and Pleasant Valley branch line was still in operation (top center). The population of Tucker rose so rapidly with the coming of the D&RGW main line that unused boxcars were put into service for housing for employees.

By 1913, the Denver and Rio Grande Western began to rework the line from Tucker to Soldier Summit to cut down the steep eastbound grade. The new line began its ascent at Detour, two miles west of Tucker, and was situated 125 feet above the canyon floor, effectively cutting off the town. Pictured here, a light engine travels the new grade outside of Tucker around 1913, marking the end of the town.

Also known as Upper Tucker, the small settlement of Gilluly was established on the Denver and Rio Grande as a water stop and section town. Gilluly maintained a spur siding for westbound trains coming down the mountain. Similar to a runaway vehicle ramp, the spur siding had an uphill grade to stop any train that needed help. This c. 1925 photograph shows a line of Utah Railway coal cars waiting behind the section houses.

The new, gentler grade between Tucker and Soldier Summit was truly a feat of engineering. The new track alignment added six miles to the main line track but kept the grade at 2.4 percent with an ingenious series of loops. This photograph, taken in 1925, shows a freight with a mid-train helper working up the grade outside of Gilluly. If an engineer's train was long enough, he could look back on it three times.

If Helper was the beginning of the Denver and Rio Grande's route through the Wasatch Mountains, then Thistle was the end. Founded in 1879 at the junction of Thistle Creek and Soldier Creek, Thistle became a major railroad town when the D&RGW laid in tracks in 1883. This c. 1900 photograph shows the railroad yards and the newly constructed Rio Grande Western Sevier Railway turning off to the left.

Rio Grande Western Engine No. 11 and her crew stop for a photograph in Thistle in 1894. Originally sold to the Denver and Rio Grande Western in 1886, No. 11 was later bought by the Rio Grande Western and eventually rebuilt to standard gauge. The engine was renumbered to No. 553 and then No. 290. A Class C-14 2-8-0 built by Baldwin in 1882, it was dismantled in 1924.

Thistle had a six-stall brick roundhouse, built in 1913, to provide helper power for the eastbound climb to Soldier Summit. As a helper station, Thistle had maintenance sheds, a water tower, a coal tower, and a large rail yard. Because of the large volume of wooden buildings, fire ravaged Thistle numerous times during the town's history and destroyed several parts of town.

Situated between the river and the railroad tracks, the Junction House served as a boardinghouse for train crews and travelers. The Junction House was run by "Uncle Bob" and "Grandma" Henderson and was known locally as Grandma Henderson's Boarding House in the 1920s. This c. 1895 photograph shows the house after the addition of a porch. (Courtesy Amanda V. Maddox.)

John William (far right) and Christiancia (second from right) Huff posed for a photograph in the Thistle rail yards c. 1918. John was the deputy sheriff and justice of the peace in Thistle from 1917 to 1925 and was shot in the Thistle rail yards when he was mistaken for a robber in March 1920. Huff was loaded onto an empty railcar and rushed to Provo, where he made a full recovery. (Courtesy Amanda V. Maddox.)

For recreation, the railroad built a resort at a natural hot spring a few miles west of Thistle. Developed in 1891, Castilla Hot Springs had an indoor and outdoor swimming pool, a hotel, and pavilions for dancing. Residents of Thistle and Soldier Summit traveled by train to the resort, where the children would play in the pools and the adults would dance the night away. (Courtesy SueAnn Martell.)

Originally from Georgia, DeWitt Tolliver Brown moved to Thistle to become a machinist on the D&RGW. Brown posed for this photograph c. 1920 in the Thistle rail yards with No. 1068, a Class L-96 2-8-8-2 built by Schenectady in 1913. No. 1068 weighed 458,000 pounds and had 95,000 pounds of tractive effort. It was renumbered 3408 and dismantled in 1951. (Courtesy Amanda V. Maddox.)

When steam was beginning to give way to diesel, Thistle began to dwindle. While Thistle maintained the rail yards for car repair and helper service, the coal tower, water tank, and roundhouse were no longer needed. This *c.* 1959 photograph shows a busy rail yard, but most of the businesses had closed, and only a handful of families were still living in the town.

The town of Thistle is gone. A short 10 years after this photograph was taken, Thistle was destroyed when a massive landslide blocked the river and flooded the town. Despite the Rio Grande's best efforts, the railroad was lost. On April 14, 1983, the westbound *California Zephyr* passed over the damaged track at 10 miles per hour—the last train to ever run through Thistle.

Five

THE SOLDIER SUMMIT EXPERIMENT

The history of Soldier Summit stretches back to the Civil War. In 1861, a small group of soldiers made camp at the summit, where a sudden snowstorm came up and stranded the group. The soldiers who died were buried where they fell, giving the area its name. A traveler passing through Soldier Summit today would see a small elevation marker and a scattering of foundations—no indication of the railroad drama that took place there.

Rumors of moving the terminal from Helper to Soldier Summit had been surfacing for some time. In 1917, talk of reducing the workday to an eight-hour shift prompted railroad officials to threaten Helper with the move, and officials hoped that the threat would keep workers from pursuing the shorter day. Helper was located too close to Green River, Utah—a short 75 miles—for an eight-hour day to be cost effective for the railroad. In 1918, the country's railroads were financially and physically falling apart. In response, the U.S. Railroad Administration formed and took over operations of all railroads. By 1919, the Helper division point was moved to Soldier Summit. The assistant general manager of the Utah line stated that during the winter "it will experience the most rigorous weather in the state." He also added that "weather conditions contribute little to the retardation of modern railroad terminals" and would result in "an interesting little city."

He was right about the interesting city but dead wrong about the weather. After several winters of severe blizzards and temperatures reaching 40 below, the Soldier Summit experiment ended when the terminal, along with all of the railroad's buildings and employee houses, were moved back to Helper. The original cost of the move was approximately $800,000, but the lessons that it taught railroad officials and the U.S. Railroad Administration about mountain railroading were priceless.

Located at an elevation of 7,440, Soldier Summit had been used as a railroad siding starting in 1882. It was not until the post–World War I debacle of the U.S. Railroad Administration that Soldier Summit became a full-fledged community and bustling railroad center. The first depot at Soldier Summit, c. 1900, was located near the siding and the turning wye so that helper engines could return to either Helper or Thistle.

By 1919, the railroad had constructed a new depot at Soldier Summit with offices for employees. While the moving of the terminal from Helper to Soldier Summit was a knee-jerk reaction by the newly formed U.S. Railroad Administration, the bad weather was the reason that the terminal was moved back to Helper. This c. 1926 photograph shows a typical Soldier Summit winter.

By 1920, the Denver and Rio Grande Railroad had begun to move division operations from Helper to Soldier Summit. This photograph taken during the winter of 1924 shows the layout of the rail yards and the volume of train traffic on the tracks. Though picturesque, the landscape and the weather did little for the efficiency of the railroad.

The railroad built five- and six-room cottages for its workers and their families right next to the rail yard so employees could get to work quickly. Soldier Summit maintained "call boys," young boys who went from house to house "calling" the crews to come to the yards and man their trains. These boys worked through the night.

These 1924 photographs show from left to right the engine house, the elevated ramp to the coal chute, the maintenance shed, and the depot. Scores of boxcars and coal cars lined the tracks waiting transport and providing fuel for road and helper engines. The nine-stall engine house was moved from Helper and reassembled at Soldier Summit, while all other buildings, including company housing and a beanery, were built new. The cost for the relocation of rail operations from Helper to Soldier Summit was a staggering $1,581,000, a princely sum for good intentions. By 1921, the town of Soldier Summit was incorporated and was reported to have over 2,500 residents.

The years leading up to World War I were turbulent ones for workers, and strikes were common. At Soldier Summit, just as in other company towns, striking workers were removed from their homes. This photograph at Soldier Summit shows striking workers living in tents across the street from the company homes. The Utah National Guard was stationed there to protect the strikers as well as the interests of the railroad. (Courtesy Amanda V. Maddox.)

The Denver and Rio Grande Railroad actively recruited men who had returned home from World War I and found it difficult to obtain work in the labor force. Many veterans returned to find that the life they left would not be enough to pay the bills. These where just three of the men who answered that call and arrived at Soldier Summit for work c. 1920.

For these new residents, life in Soldier Summit revolved around the railroad. In this *c.* 1929 photograph, sisters Evelyn and Alice Maddox play with their baby dolls just off the railroad yards next to the beanery. The employee cottages are shown on the opposite side of the tracks. (Courtesy Amanda V. Maddox.)

Moving from a farm in Hinckley, Utah, Irene Greener and her children Virginia and Jim came to Soldier Summit with her husband, James A. Greener. James and his brother Ray worked in the car maintenance department. This *c.* 1924 photograph was taken on the front porch of their home. (Courtesy SueAnn Martell.)

During the harsh winters at Soldier Summit, paths had to be dug to the outhouse. Here, from left to right, Jim Greener, Ruth Carlquist, and Virginia Greener play in the snow on that path. Often the child of a railroader would grow up to be a railroader as well. Jim Greener grew up to be the Utah Division Superintendent for the Denver and Rio Grande Western. (Courtesy SueAnn Martell.)

This is how Soldier Summit's Main Street looked c. 1920. The bulk of the businesses were located on the left side of the street, while the railroad housing was located on the right. The rail yards are out of sight behind the homes. Although greatly improved, this is the same stretch of road that today's travelers use to drive through town.

An unidentified locomotive leads a freight train into the Soldier Summit rail yards, while a railroad worker rests against a handcar c. 1928. In the mid-1920s, the railroad built a viaduct over the rail yards to offer the town's residents safer passage from one side of town to the other without them having to cross over numerous sets of tracks in the busy yard.

The area of Soldier Summit north of Main Street featured additional houses, a rough baseball field where the town team played during the summer, and the new six-room schoolhouse (right), built in 1921 at a cost of $30,000. By 1922, the school had over 200 students, from elementary to high school, and five full-time teachers.

The winters were cruel in Soldier Summit. Unlike other high mountain areas of the Denver and Rio Grande Western, Soldier Summit was located in a high, wide valley. Once the snow fell, the wind came and blew it into deep drifts. For the many railroaders who were responsible for keeping the main line open, a Soldier Summit blizzard was quite an experience. The depot is pictured here in 1926 during a blizzard.

The two-story depot at Soldier Summit was nearly buried during the winter of 1924. Railroader Carroll Maddox posed in front of the building to show the depth of the snow—a striking photograph with the elevation of the town clearly marked on the sign at the depot. Residents were forced to dig enclosed tunnels to their outhouses and coal sheds while the railroad struggled to keep the main line open. (Courtesy Amanda V. Maddox.)

The same 1924 blizzard buried the Soldier Summit Post Office to the roof. It was necessary to build a tunnel through the snow to access the front door. The weather made living conditions miserable for residents. Coal for the company houses traveled by train from Helper in open cars and was frozen solid by the time it reached Soldier Summit. (Courtesy Amanda V. Maddox.)

The heavy snow made it difficult to keep the rail yards—and even the main line from Helper to Provo—open during the winter months. This 1924 photograph shows Denver and Rio Grande Western spreader No. 44 put into service as a snowplow to clear the tracks in the Soldier Summit yards. Car man James A. Greener is operating the blade. (Courtesy SueAnn Martell.)

This locomotive ran through a few drifts on its way to Soldier Summit in 1924. Note the deep snow, colored by coal dust and piled up around the rails. In 1924, the Denver and Rio Grande Western Railroad renumbered the majority of its locomotives. Locomotives with the new numbers were also relettered "D&RGW" to reflect the railroad's reorganization. (Courtesy SueAnn Martell.)

An eastbound passenger train works up a full head of steam out of Soldier Summit during a blizzard in 1926. Many of the residents of Soldier Summit came to enjoy the remoteness of the area; however, visitors were surprised to find a town situated on the top of a mountain.

Even after the age of steam, snow removal was still required on Soldier Summit. Here Engine No. 3076, an EMD 3,000 horsepower GP40, pushes snowplow No. 44 just outside of Soldier Summit around 1969. This same type of spreader/snowplow is on display at the Western Mining and Railroad Museum in Helper; it was retired from service by the Union Pacific.

By the mid-1920s, based on its population and infrastructure, Soldier Summit was ranked as a third-class city in Utah with nearly 3,000 residents. Even though the railroad would pull the operations out of Soldier Summit four years later and the population would take a drastic downturn, the town continued to survive and was still used by the railroad as a turnaround and section town. This c. 1925 photograph shows the town at its peak.

This c. 1921 photograph shows the Summit Café and the Soldier Summit Lumber Company. In 1919, a real estate company took interest in Soldier Summit and was determined to make a "real town" out of the land. While the town had its ups and downs, Soldier Summit remained an incorporated town until the late 1970s, when Wasatch County dissolved the town against the wishes of the handful of residents.

Taken from the behind the schoolhouse, this 1926 photograph shows the bustling railroad yards and the large groupings of railroad houses. When the railroad abandoned the hope of a division point at Soldier Summit, it moved the employee homes to Helper, placing them near the railroad yards. Today many of these homes remain in Helper.

The engine house and the maintenance buildings were carefully torn down and moved to Helper in 1929. For the engine house, this was its second move—once from Helper to Soldier Summit and then from Soldier Summit back to Helper. Here D&RGW Crane No. 0131 removes a large section of the roof of the engine house as the railroad workers prepare for the journey back to Helper.

With pieces of concrete lying nearby and no walls to the building, Engine No. 3502 was the last locomotive to leave the engine house at Soldier Summit. No. 3502 was a huge Class L-107 2-8-8-2 built by Richmond in 1923. It had 57-inch drivers, weighed 534,000 pounds, and had 107,374 pounds of tractive effort. The locomotive was dismantled in 1947.

During the 1920s, Soldier Summit boasted a theater for movies, dozens of stores, several churches, and a wide variety of restaurants. Though many of the businesses left with the railroad in 1929, several remained. Pictured here in 1937 are, from left to right, Takae Nakamura, Clara Valate Brown, and Norma Lewis, standing in front of the theater on their way home from school. (Courtesy Amanda V. Maddox.)

For the people who stayed on at Soldier Summit, life on top of their mountain continued at a more leisurely pace. Trains still rumbled through town, but the excitement of the busy rail yard had moved to Helper. Sitting on one of the vacant foundations, young Clara Valate Brown shows off her guitar-playing and singing skills for some of the town's residents. (Courtesy Amanda V. Maddox.)

WESTWARD · MAIN LINE · EASTWARD

17 California Zephyr Leave Daily	7 Prospector Leave Daily	Mile Posts	Capacity of Siding		STATIONS — Sub-Division 6 — TIME-TABLE No. 138 — APRIL 24, 1955	Station Numbers	Capacity of Siding	Miles from Salt Lake	18 California Zephyr Arrive Daily	8 Prospector Arrive Daily
7 08 PM	5 15 AM	626.4	Yard	Ra	HELPER BK	9032	Yard	119.7	8 43 AM	8 35 PM
					2.4					
7 13	5 21	628.8	68		UTAH RY. JCT. j	9038	68	117.3	8 37	8 26
					1.6					
7 16	5 24	630.4	Yard		CASTLE GATE w	9044	Yard	115.7	8 34	8 23
7 19	5 27	631.6			ROYAL	9046	76	114.5	8 31	8 20
					3.5					
7 28	5 36	635.1	85		NOLAN	9048	82	111.0	8 24	8 13
					3.8					
7 35	5 44	638.9	102	kn	KYUNE DNWY	9050	102	107.2	8 17	8 05
7 43	5 54	644.4	92		COLTON JWY	9054	Yard	101.7	8 09	7 56
					7.0					
7 51	f 6 02	651.4	Yard	jf	SOLDIER SUMMIT DNWY	9056	105	94.7	8 01	f 7 47
					9.6					
8 08	6 21	661.0	105		GILLULY w	9060	62	85.1	7 45	7 27
					4.6					
8 15	6 31	665.6			DETOUR	9062	103	80.5	7 37	7 19
					6.6					
8 25	6 41	672.2	107		NARROWS	9066	116	73.9	7 29	7 09
					4.3					
8 32	6 49	676.5			RIO	9068	108	69.6	7 22	7 02
					4.4					
8 39	s 6 56	680.9	117	Jd	THISTLE DNBFJKSWY	9070	123	65.2	7 15	s 6 55
					3.6					
8 43	7 01	684.5			CASTILLA	9076	71	61.6	7 11	6 48
					4.1					
		688.6			GOMEX	9078		57.5		
					7.2 / 2.1					
					SUTRO	9082	71	55.4		6 41
					6.1 (Eastward)					
8 55	f 7 15	695.8		Ng	SPRINGVILLE DJW	9302		49.3	6 58	f 6 34
					3.1					
		698.9			U. P. CROSSING			46.2		
					2.2					
s 9 05 PM	s 7 28	701.1	108	vo	PROVO DNBFJKOSWY	9310	107	44.0	s 6 52 AM	s 6 27 PM
					4.6					
		705.7			U. P. CROSSING			39.4		
					1.5					
		707.2			GENEVA	9317		37.9		
					1.2					
		708.4			DERN			36.7		
					5.3					
		713.7	257	Af	AMERICAN FORK	9321	257	31.4		
					3.3					
		717.0			LEHI	9324		28.1		
					3.3					
		720.3	104		MESA	9325	104	24.8		
					2.5					
		722.8			NASH	9326		22.3		
					2.7					
		725.5	105		OLIVERS	9327	105	19.6		
					3.1					
		728.6	158		RIVERTON	9328	158	16.5		
					4.0					
		732.6			ENDOT	9329		12.5		
					1.9					
		734.5	Yard	Bj	MIDVALE DJWT	9332	143	10.6		
					3.9					
		738.4	Yard		MURRAY	9336	39	6.7		
					2.3					
9 45 PM	8 17 AM	740.7			EAST ROPER	9350		4.4		
					1.8					
9 47	8 19	742.5	Yard	ry	ROPER BK	9350	Yard	2.6	6 06 AM	5 36 PM
					1.7					
		744.2			U. P. CROSSING			0.9		
					0.9					
10 00 PM	8 30 AM	745.1	Yard	Un	SALT LAKE CITY BK	6000	Yard		6 00 AM	5 30 PM
Arrive Daily	Arrive Daily				(119.7)				Leave Daily	Leave Daily
2.52 / 41.4	3.15 / 36.5				Schedule Time / Average Speed per Hour				2.43 / 44.1	3.05 / 38.9

Trains operate by Centralized Traffic Control in east end of Helper Yard; on westward main track between A. B. S. 6347W, Nolan, and A. B. S. 6388 Kyune; between westward A. B. S. 7013W and 7013E, Provo, and eastward A. B. S. 7408W, 7408E, 7408WF and 7408EF, East Roper.

This timetable for the Salt Lake Division was issued on April 24, 1955. It shows the arrival and departure times for the eastbound and westbound *California Zephyr* and the D&RGW *Prospector*. The timetable states that all freight trains are required to stop at Soldier Summit and test their air brakes. This rule came on the heels of an accident just west of Soldier Summit near the siding of Scenic. In the mid-1940s, the westbound No. 5 *Exposition Flyer* left Soldier Summit and headed down toward Gilluly when the engineer tried to set the train's air to slow their speed. The air brakes failed to set, and the speeding engine broke free from the lead baggage car, tumbling over the embankment. Thankfully no passengers were hurt, but unfortunately the engineer was killed in the accident. (Courtesy SueAnn Martell.)

Six

Branch Lines
to the Hub

While the Denver and Rio Grande Western had little interest in pursuing branch or spur lines, the area's vital coal industry made the short lines a necessity. Beginning with the purchase of the Utah and Pleasant Valley Railroad line, the D&RGW slowly began to act as a wealthy "big brother" to these smaller, local lines. With that purchase, they secured their place as the dominant coal hauler in the area.

That title was challenged with the formation of the Kenilworth and Helper Railroad. The plans for the Kenilworth and Helper Railroad were grand. When the line was initially founded, the plan was to take the route all of the way to Vernal near the Colorado border and connect it to the Uintah Railway. However, with the steep grades and the slow equipment, the railroad soon could not keep up with the demand for coal transport. Again, the D&RGW stepped in and offered to operate the railroad for the Independent Coal and Coke Company. While the railroad never did expand past Kenilworth, the larger railroad made the route profitable.

The branch line through Spring Canyon was nearly the end of the Denver and Grande Western's coal-hauling days. Fighting off its own financial troubles and facing a hungrier smaller competitor in the Utah Railway, the Denver and Rio Grande Western was forced to share the right-of-way in order to keep some of the local coal business in the canyon.

The railroad found out that these branch lines, located deep in the heart of coal country, were a necessary evil for a successful business. Radiating out like spokes from a wheel, these branch lines served as arteries to the main line of the Denver and Rio Grande Western and made Helper the hub of Utah's coal industry.

Three years after the completion of the original Utah and Pleasant Valley Railroad, the Denver and Rio Grande Western Railroad bought the line to secure control of the area and the coal traffic. In late 1882, the D&RGW constructed a new line to the mines of Pleasant Valley, stretching from Colton to Clear Creek with a spur to Winter Quarters. This 1882 photograph shows the crew constructing the new line.

The town of Scofield was named after C. W. Scofield, director of the Utah and Pleasant Valley Railroad from 1880 to 1882. The town served as a small division point and was used to route coal cars to and from the neighboring mines. A section crew works on the multiple lines in Scofield in 1900.

The Pleasant Valley line traveled up the canyon from Scofield to the mines at Winter Quarters. The mine and the town were owned by the Utah Fuel Company, a subsidiary of the Denver and Rio Grande Western Railroad. In this c. 1890 photograph, the miners at Winter Quarters pose with their mules and horses for a photograph near the four-track tipple before they enter the mine to work.

E. Schuman's bridge crew was captured on film by photographer G. E. Anderson at Hales in 1903. Hales was a small section town constructed on the new Pleasant Valley line from Colton to Scofield. The families of the bridge crew lived in the railcars until housing could be built. The line at Hales was rebuilt in 1925 to allow for the construction of the Scofield Reservoir.

The Denver and Rio Grande provided passenger service on the Pleasant Valley line for the towns of Scofield, Winter Quarters, and Clear Creek. In this *c.* 1909 photograph, two unidentified locomotives pull five baggage cars and a least six passenger cars between Pleasant Valley Junction (Colton) and Hales. For many immigrants coming to work at the coal mines, this was their transportation into town.

Just east of Helper, the small coal mining town of Kenilworth was founded in 1906. Discouraged by the railroad's domination of the coal industry, Independent Coal and Coke Company began the mining operations and built its own railroad, the Kenilworth and Helper. This *c.* 1911 photograph shows the Kenilworth and Helper No. 150, a Y-40 Shay geared locomotive built for steep grades. Built by Lima, No. 150 weighed 203,000 pounds and had 40,397 pounds of tractive effort.

Situated in a high mountain valley, the town of Kenilworth was difficult to get to, especially for a railroad. The Kenilworth and Helper Railroad was a 3.75-mile-long standard-gauge road with a staggering 6.1-percent grade from Independent Junction to the mine tipple. This overhead view of Kenilworth around 1930 shows the mine tipple (lower left) and the neat rows of company houses stretching out below it.

This c. 1911 photograph shows an early tipple at Kenilworth with a variety of boxcars and coal cars waiting at the bottom. The small cars overturned near the tracks are the mine cars, which were used to load coal in the mine, move the coal down the tramway, and load it on to the tipple, where it was sorted and loaded into the railroad cars.

The little Shay engines owned by the Kenilworth and Helper Railroad were great for steep climbing, but they were also slow moving. After operating for nearly three years, the Kenilworth and Helper could not keep up with the financial burdens of the road. The Denver and Rio Grande Western Railroad took over operations of the line for the lease of the equipment. This *c.* 1912 photograph shows one of the sure-footed little Shays on a wooden trestle bridge just outside of Kenilworth.

The Denver and Rio Grande Western Railroad continued to operate the Kenilworth and Helper line until 1926, when the demand for coal became greater than the speed at which the small Shays could travel. This *c.* 1916 photograph shows a leased Shay engine with a wide mix of boxcars under the Kenilworth tipple. A loaded mine car sits on top of the tipple. The mine tramway ran nearly vertical (center right) up the mountain side.

In 1926, the Denver and Rio Grande Western abandoned the Kenilworth and Helper Railroad and built its own line to Kenilworth. Leaving the main line at north Helper, the new line traveled along the base of the mountain and into Kenilworth on a much gentler grade. This allowed the D&RGW to use its larger locomotives and the Shays were sold. This *c.* 1930 photograph shows the new Kenilworth tipple and the steep mine tramway (left center).

The Spring Canyon Branch of the Denver and Rio Grande Western was constructed in 1913. It left the main line in south Helper and traveled west to the mining towns of Peerless, Spring Canyon, Standardville, Latuda, Rains, Mutual, and Little Standard—a distance of nearly 11 miles. This *c.* 1912 photograph shows the construction of the branch swinging west just off the main line.

Although the coal seam at Peerless was approximately 18 inches thick, the mining company was producing a lot of coal for its markets. The peak of the coal activity occurred in the 1920s, and a shortage of railroad cars to transport the coal on the Denver and Rio Grande Western angered the mine owners. This c. 1918 photograph shows the town of Peerless with the tipple at the center of town. The D&RGW tracks are shown running under the tipple.

By 1920, the mines of lower Spring Canyon had reached the end of their rope with the Denver and Rio Grande Western, and thus the Utah Railway's Utah Terminal line was born. The Utah's branch line paralleled D&RGW's line through the canyon and served the three coal mines. This 1929 photograph of the Spring Canyon Coal Company tipple shows the Utah Terminal lines on the left and the single D&RGW line on the far right.

The final coal camp on the Utah Terminal line was Standardville. Opened in 1912 by F. A. Sweet, Standardville was designed to be the "standard" of all future coal mine camps. With landscaped lawns and open areas, the town also boasted numerous shops, a school, and a hospital. This c. 1930 photograph shows the amusement hall (left) and the large cement tipple (right). Utah Coal Route railcars are lined up next to the tipple.

With two railroads operating in a narrow canyon, Spring Canyon was a busy place for rail traffic. Joe Saccomano eased Denver and Rio Grande Western Locomotive No. 3500 down the canyon past Standardville in this c. 1928 photograph. No. 3500 was a Class L-107 2-8-8-2 built by Richmond in 1923. The large locomotive weighed 534,000 pounds with 107,374 pounds of tractive effort. It was dismantled in October 1951.

The unique operation of the Standardville tipple is seen in this publicity photograph from 1912. Tipple workers and mine officials pose for the photograph while the tipple mechanism tips the D&RGW car up on the rotor to unload it. Standardville mine foreman Thomas Lamph stands in the center of the group.

Although the Denver and Rio Grande Western lost some of its coal business on the Spring Canyon branch line to the Utah Railway, they still provided service to the upper canyon coal camps of Latuda, Rains, Mutual, and Little Standard. In this c. 1920 photograph, two loaded coal cars wait to be picked up by the D&RGW for transport down the canyon.

Located approximately half a mile west of Rains, the town of Mutual was the last camp to be opened in Spring Canyon. Although the mine only produced coal for 17 years, the camp peaked at 250 residents, many of which worked at neighboring coal camps. This *c.* 1925 photograph shows the tipple at Mutual after a snowstorm.

The Spring Canyon branch was not immune to accidents on either railroad. This spectacular crash on the Utah Railway side of the canyon, just west of the Utah Railway steel bridge, killed one railroader and created a disastrous mess. Local residents drove up the canyon to watch the cleanup efforts along the track. The D&RGW Spring Canyon line is in the foreground of this *c.* 1955 photograph.

Another view, *c.* 1955, of the same Utah Railway accident shows the twisted metal of the Utah Coal Route cars and the locomotive turned on her side. The steep grade of the Spring Canyon branch made runaways common and brake failure a scary possibility. It was necessary to clean up the coal and try to salvage as much of it as possible in an effort to minimize the financial loss to the rail company.

A similar accident occurred on the Denver and Rio Grande Western Spring Canyon branch *c.* 1915. This tangled mess of coal cars and piles of coal near Peerless was probably the result of a runaway. Another accident on the line occurred when a crew left their train unattended in the town of Spring Canyon. The train left without them and traveled all the way to Helper, where it hit another train and rolled over in a hay field.

Seven

DEPRESSION
AND RECOVERY

When a town depends solely on industry, prosperity is very cyclical. Since 1881, Helper has experienced both ups and downs. Coal mining was seasonal and only truly reliable during the fall and winter months, and farming was difficult. Labor struggles plagued both the railroad and the coal industry.

During the 1920s, the country was living the high life. Work was plentiful and the local coal mines were at a peak production period. Helper experienced a building boom, and the Denver and Rio Grande Western could not keep up the demand from the mines.

By the 1930s, the good times were gone. The country was in the death grip of the Great Depression, work was scarce, and coal mines began to shut down. But with all of the sorrow of the era, the railroad industry and consequently Helper itself continued to grow thanks to the relocation of the Soldier Summit terminal. The Works Project Administration built numerous structures in town, and Helper survived.

During the 1940s, World War II raged, and once again, the railroads and the coal mines reached another peak in production. Soon advances in technology would change the face of railroading forever with the introduction of the electric diesel locomotive. These machines, though efficient, cost jobs, and the area was once again put into a downward trend.

It was once said that when the apocalypse comes the only things to survive will be cockroaches and Helper, Utah. That may be true as Helper, the Denver and Rio Grande Western, and the Utah Railway have certainly experienced their fair share of depression and recovery.

A group of Denver and Rio Grande Western articulated locomotives pulled out the engine house in Helper for a photograph *c.* 1929. Three of the engines are, from left to right, Nos. 1063, 1073, and 1060. All three are Class L-96 2-8-8-2 built by Schenectady in 1913. They weighed 458,000 pounds with 95,000 pounds of tractive effort. The fourth engine is unidentified but probably of the same series.

Although the railroad moved the majority of its operations to Soldier Summit in 1919, Helper never faltered but acted a commercial center to the surrounding coal camps. This 1920 photograph shows the south end of Helper's Main Street. The three-story Helper Hotel, an upscale hotel for newly arriving immigrants and the current home to the Western Mining and Railroad Museum, is visible in the center of the photograph.

Having a seat on a steaming locomotive's boiler must have seemed like a good idea at the time for the Helper maintenance crew in this *c.* 1925 photograph. The Helper yard maintained the helper engines for the return trip to Soldier Summit. Even though the division point had been moved to the top of the mountain, the local coal trains still had to make a 2.4-percent climb out of Castle Gate.

Rio Grande Locomotive No. 1501, a Class M-67 4-8-2 built by Brooks in 1922, sits in the Helper yard around 1926. No. 1501 had 66,640 pounds of tractive effort with 63-inch drivers. Weighing 377,000 pounds, with 210 pounds of boiler pressure, it was dismantled in 1954.

During the 1920s, the United States enacted the Prohibition Act, which banned the consumption, production, and sale of alcohol. With the large immigrant population in Helper, Prohibition did little to close the saloons that lined Main Street. In this *c.* 1921 photograph at the 66 Saloon, the bartender did not look too concerned about the alcohol inspectors showing up in his bar that day.

Italian immigrant John "Jack" Marchello (right) worked on the Denver and Rio Grande Western Railroad as a fireman and, in the Italian tradition, made his own wine. In this *c.* 1924 photograph, Marchello posed for the camera at a local Helper bar where he sold his wine. While alcohol inspectors did their best to enforce the law, it was nearly impossible to catch all of the violations. (Courtesy SueAnn Martell.)

Denver and Rio Grande Western No. 3611 provided helper power, tucked in front of the caboose, for a fully loaded Utah Coal Route train as it left the Helper yard c. 1930. No. 3611 was a Class L-132 2-8-8-2 built by Schenectady in 1930. It weighed a whopping 665,000 pounds and had 63-inch drivers and 131,800 pounds of tractive effort.

By the mid-1930s, the United States was firmly in the grip of the Great Depression. Helper used the decade of the 1930s to restate its position as Utah's industrial center. This arch, pictured here in 1934, greeted visitors who traveled into Helper. The pillars were made of coal and the entire arch was lighted at night. Ironically the arch was knocked down in the 1950s when it was hit by a coal truck.

In the 1930s, Helper had several furniture stores, six grocery stores, scores of restaurants, and other businesses. Pictured here *c.* 1930 are, from left to right, the O. K. Lunch, O. K. Tailors, O. P. Skaggs Grocery, and the Helper Furniture Store. Above the Helper Furniture Store was the Hotel Utah. This hotel served as the home base for Utah National Guard troops when they were called to the area during labor strikes.

Helper's Main Street was a busy place by the mid-1930s. Pictured here *c.* 1934 are, from left to right, Newhouse Hotel, Avalon Hotel, Grill Café, Colonial Hotel, Barboglio Bakery and Hotel, Lowenstein Mercantile, and Golden Gate Cabaret. Aside from its bustling Main Street, Helper participated in the Works Project Administration Program, which built several structures in town, including a new junior high school.

At the height of the Depression, as part of the 1934 Labor Day celebration, Helper City flooded the street and filled it with fish. Children were allowed to catch the fish and keep what they caught. The son of an Italian immigrant, eight-year-old George Martell proudly displayed the fish he caught. When asked what the Depression was like Martell responded, "We were poor but it didn't matter we were poor anyway." (Courtesy SueAnn Martell.)

The beautiful Denver and Rio Grande Western No. 3703 paused in Helper for a photograph *c.* 1938. No. 3703 was a Class L-105 4-6-6-4 built by Baldwin in 1938. It weighed 620,000 pounds, had 105,000 pounds of tractive effort, and had 70-inch drivers. Wrecked on October 19, 1952, in a boiler explosion, it was dismantled in 1955.

Denver and Rio Grande Western Railroad No. 3303 steams into the Helper yards headed eastbound in 1939. No. 3303 was originally No. 1053, a Class L-62 2-6-6-2 built by Schenectady in 1910. It weighed 340,000 pounds and had 62,026 pounds of tractive effort and 200 pounds of boiler pressure. It was dismantled in 1950. (Courtesy SueAnn Martell.)

Huge Rio Grande Locomotive No. 3710 was photographed in the Helper yards near the coal tower shortly after it was delivered in 1942. No. 3710 was a Baldwin Class L-105 4-6-6-4 weighing 641,700 pounds with 105,000 pounds of tractive effort on 70-inch drivers. During World War II, the War Production Board diverted an additional six of these behemoths from the Union Pacific to the Rio Grande. (Courtesy SueAnn Martell.)

Denver and Rio Grande Western Locomotive No. 1608 waited in the Helper yard *c.* 1940. No. 1608 was a Baldwin Class M-75 4-8-2. It weighed 419,310 pounds with 74,970 pounds of tractive effort on 67-inch drivers and 210 pounds of boiler pressure. In 1948, the locomotive was dismantled. (Courtesy SueAnn Martell.)

No. 3500 sat ready near the Spring Canyon branch waiting for a mine run *c.* 1940. No. 3500, a 2-8-8-2, was suited to handle the heavily loaded coal trains up and down the steep grades. Engineers who ran these large machines reported that they were more like living creatures than machines. If they were handled properly and respected, they were good to the crew. (Courtesy SueAnn Martell.)

Denver and Rio Grande Western No. 1713, a Class M-64 4-8-4 built by Baldwin in 1929, sits in the Helper yard after being torn up by a main rod failure c. 1945. Note how the main rod sliced into the boiler. No. 1713 weighed 418,150 pounds with 63,700 pounds of tractive effort. It was repaired after the accident and was not dismantled until 1955.

No one ever said that railroad work was always hard. This photograph from 1941 shows, from left to right, an unidentified worker, Joe Saccomano, Cliff Hansen, Bill Murphy, and another unidentified worker sitting on Engine No. 3504. They were doing some repair work and spinning a few tall railroad tales. No. 3504 was a Richmond Class L-107 2-8-8-2.

Denver and Rio Grande Western No. 3800 was one of six Class L-97 4-6-6-4 Challengers built by Schenectady in 1943. The engines weighed 627,000 pounds and had 69-inch drivers. All six were sold in 1947 to the Clinchfield Railroad. No. 3800 had her photograph taken in Salt Lake City on her way to Helper in 1943.

A car man uses a nearby signal light to gain some height next to Denver and Rio Grande Western No. 3713 while he performs some final repairs c. 1944. No. 3713 was a Baldwin Class L-105 4-6-6-4 weighing 641,700 pounds with 105,000 pounds of tractive effort. It was dismantled in 1954. The nose of No. 3713 shows the stripe pattern used during and immediately after World War II.

The car and maintenance departments in Helper have always been first-class departments. In 1948, the workers and office staff posed in front of the Rio Grande coal car to show that the shop had garnered an award by operating 3,722 days since the last reportable accident. In the late 1960s, the car department earned another safety award at 5,840 days without a reportable accident. In the above photograph, car foreman James A. Greener is third from right in back row. Pictured below directly behind the sign are Cedo Cavannini (left) and George Martell. Car men earned the name "car toads" because of the strange stooped over hopping walk they used when inspecting cars. (Both courtesy SueAnn Martell.)

GOOD ONLY OVER DIVISION ON WHICH ISSUED

The Denver and Rio Grande Western Railroad Company

NOT GOOD ON ZEPHYR TRAINS

TRIP PASS　　　　　K 10329

(SUBJECT TO CONDITIONS ON BACK)

PASS George A. Martell — —

ACCOUNT Carman Helper

FROM Salt Lake City, Ut. TO Helper, Utah

ISSUED 2 May 1949　　　　EXPIRES 2 July 1949

ADDRESS Helper, Utah　　REQUESTED BY RHB

VALID WHEN COUNTERSIGNED BY

COUNTERSIGNED BY *A. F. Thayer*　　*Wilson McCarthy*

PRESIDENT

Passes issued to the employee covered their immediate family for trips. This trip pass was issued to Helper car man George Martell on May 2, 1949. Valid from Salt Lake City to Helper, it was good on any train but the *Zephyr*. The pass was signed by A. F. Thayer and stamped by Denver and Rio Grande president Wilson McCarthy. (Courtesy SueAnn Martell.)

Rio Grande Locomotive No. 3561 spent some of her last days working out of Helper. This *c.* 1946 photograph shows the locomotive attached to a freight with the dramatic Book Cliffs in the background. Locomotive No. 3561 was a Class L-109 2-8-8-2 built by Baldwin. It was part of 15 engines purchased by the D&RGW from the Norfolk and Western in May 1945. Built in 1919, No. 3561 was dismantled in 1947.

Sitting near the sand tower in the Helper yard, Rio Grande No. 3603, a Class L-131 2-8-8-2 built by Brooks in 1927, waits for her next run. Weighing 649,000 pounds, No. 3603 had 131,800 pounds of tractive effort and 240 pounds of boiler pressure. It was dismantled in October 1955.

In the 1950s, steam was being replaced by diesel. In this c. 1955 photograph, steam engine No. 3610 provides helper power westbound out of Helper with two pairs of F7s. No. 3610 was a Schenectady 2-8-8-2 Class L-132 built in 1930. It weighed 665,000 pounds and had 131,800 pounds of tractive effort. No. 3610 was dismantled the next year.

Car man Rudy Bruno stood in front of the Helper roundhouse just before it was demolished c. 1959. Once the proud symbol of Helper's rail power, the roundhouse had become obsolete with the introduction of diesel power. Railroader's who had worked there for years looked on in amazement as the first diesel engine rolled into Helper.

A sad sight for all steam fans was the demolition of the beautiful locomotives. Pictured here in 1952, Engine No. 3361 is being cut up for scrap in the yard at Helper. All useable materials were salvaged. Demolition of these wonderful machines signaled the end of a great era in railroading.

Two different eras met in this *c.* 1957 photograph. Two unidentified steam locomotives power up to provide helper power for a Carbon County Railway coal train while an "A" and "B" FT pair pass on the opposite track. The Rio Grande had a large fleet of the FTs, and they were used on the *Prospector* that ran between Denver and Salt Lake City.

Once the diesels became standard operating procedure, longtime railroaders had to learn a new way of railroading. Pictured here in 1960 are a group of F7 "B" units that derailed in the Helper yard when the train split a switch. The Helper wrecker crew did not have to travel far to help and got right to work to get the train up and running.

"A" unit No. 5711 was cut away from the damaged "B" unit in the Helper yard when the train split a switch. No. 5711 was a 1,500-horsepower F7 built in 1952. It was sold to the Alaska Railroad in 1970 and was renumbered 1520. The Denver and Rio Grande had 88 of the F7 "A" and "B" units in operation throughout their lines.

The eastbound *California Zephyr*, headed by Engine No. 5771, stopped in Helper to pick up passengers, to change crews, and for some service by the Helper car department *c.* 1960. No. 5771 was an F9 EMD that provided 7,000 horsepower with both the "A" and "B" units. Though the age of steam was over, an equally exciting era continued until the *California Zephyr* was discontinued in 1983.

Visit us at
arcadiapublishing.com

Printed in the USA
CPSIA information can be obtained
at www.ICGtesting.com
LVHW071539171123
764118LV00008B/802